bkac

— THE —

Astrological
Grimoire

—— THE ——

Astrological Grimoire

Timeless Horoscopes,
Modern Rituals,
and Creative Altars
for Self-Discovery

SHEWOLFE AND
BEATRIX GRAVESGUARD

CHRONICLE BOOKS
SAN FRANCISCO

Library of Congress Cataloging-in-Publication Data available.

ISBN: 978-1-4521-7086-2

Manufactured in China

Design by Anne Kenady

10 9 8 7 6 5 4 3 2 1

Chronicle books and gifts are available at special quantity discounts
to corporations, professional associations, literacy programs, and other
organizations. For details and discount information, please contact our
corporate/premiums department at corporatesales@chroniclebooks.com
or at 1-800-759-0190.

Chronicle Books LLC
680 Second Street
San Francisco, California 94107
www.chroniclebooks.com

CONTENTS

Introduction 7

Astrology Basics 11

THE SIGNS 12

ELEMENTS AND QUALITIES 14

WHAT'S IN A BIRTH CHART? 16

The Moon 18
The Houses 20
The Planets 22

DECIPHERING YOUR BIRTH CHART 24

HOW TO USE THIS BOOK 27

The Signs 31

About the Witches 200
Notes of Gratitude 201

Introduction

Time is both linear and cyclical, and growth is an ongoing process that often loops back on itself. For millennia, humans have used the seasons, the phases of the moon, and the movements of celestial objects as steady beacons as we barreled forward in time, learning to recognize patterns and to shape our futures from past mistakes. Our internal lives are also lived in these rhythms; as we shift and grow, we are given endless opportunities to evolve our relationships to our former, discarded selves.

Astrology as a divinatory practice has often been relegated to dusty New Age bookshelves, but it has re-entered popular culture as an inclusive and intersectional tool for self-reflection, as part of a growing DIY spiritualism that a new generation is turning to in the face of uncertain times. In an era where few things remain constant, the night sky is a reliable presence with a powerful narrative, eternally reminding us of the vast and awe-inspiring mysteries of the universe and our deep subatomic kinship with its beginnings.

Astrology reminds us that our lives are shaped by our surrounding influences—seen or unseen, rationally sound or scientifically unexplained. In this book, we use it as a lens to understanding ourselves and our relationships with the world, and as a perennial handbook for navigating life events and accessing our creative energies. We designed this book so that it can be used as a field guide, a blueprint, and a grimoire—a witch's sacred notebook. We aim to make it simple and intuitive to understand the twelve signs of the zodiac, which function as a layer of personality and insight on top of the calendar seasons. We've crafted our own interpretations of the signs, which attempt to discard some of the more outdated and culturally biased notions of the traditional definitions. We also recognize that systems like astrology tend to breed favor toward some signs over others, so we'll explain how all of the signs are equally significant factors in your story—not just the one you get assigned on your birthday.

The exercises in this book are devised to get you in conversation with your intuition. Many of them invite you to write or draw in order to tap into the quiet compass inside you that is pulled by a multitude of influences. They can be revisited again and again, and in doing so, we can get a glimpse of the ways we change and the ways we struggle. Feeling lost or uncertain is a huge reason why many of us are pulled toward systems and structures like astrology, looking for clear indicators and giant neon signs declaring a firm YES or NO. The magic often lies in this: You already know the answer to the questions you are asking. But due to fears, old narratives, and pressure from friends, family, and society, we learn to second-guess our desires, our dreams, our truths. Astrology can be a device for investigating what resonates and what you are in conflict with, an organizing principle that brings you back into alignment with yourself. This is your invitation to dig deeper.

A NOTE ON MATERIALS

We strongly believe in the accessible nature and ease of all the exercises provided in this book, and we don't want you to buy into a new lifestyle or aesthetic, or to spend any money that you wouldn't already. The only thing you need to have to use this book, other than your intentional self, is a pen, paper, and the occasional household item. The rituals we tend toward ourselves are nondenominational, practical, and minimal in terms of materials; all altar notes are suggestions only, and left up to your interpretation. While traditional ritual items like crystals, tarot cards, candles, etc. are magic(k)al indeed, they hold only the power we give them and are not necessary for anything we've included in this book. You can imbue any object already in your possession with the energy you require.

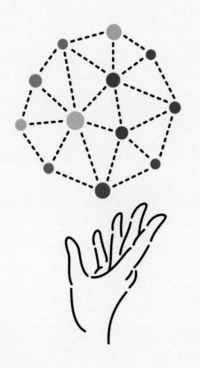

ASTROLOGY —
BASICS

The Signs

This book uses the zodiac constellations of the western astrological system, that divide up the calendar into twelve roughly equal segments. Many people's familiarity with astrology extends only to their sun sign—that is, the one corresponding to their birthday. In traditional systems, the signs are attributed to personality traits; a very introductory breakdown is below.

	SIGN	DATES*
♈	ARIES	Mar 21—Apr 20
♉	TAURUS	Apr 20—May 21
♊	GEMINI	May 21—Jun 21
♋	CANCER	Jun 21—Jul 24
♌	LEO	Jul 24—Aug 23
♍	VIRGO	Aug 23—Sep 23
♎	LIBRA	Sep 23—Oct 23
♏	SCORPIO	Oct 23—Nov 23
♐	SAGITTARIUS	Nov 23—Dec 22
♑	CAPRICORN	Dec 22—Jan 20
♒	AQUARIUS	Jan 20—Feb 19
♓	PISCES	Feb 19—Mar 21

* Note that these dates are approximate—the exact date ranges vary slightly from year to year. If you are born on or near the boundaries of two signs, your birth chart will determine which side you land on—see pages 16–17 for more.

TRAITS

Energetic, brave, aggressive, impulsive

Devoted, patient, stubborn, slothful

Curious, witty, mercurial, inconsistent

Nurturing, sensitive, moody, protective

Generous, playful, dramatic, egotistic

Analytical, meticulous, critical, reserved

Diplomatic, social, indecisive, indulgent

Magnetic, intense, secretive, possessive

Adventurous, honest, idealistic, flighty

Ambitious, disciplined, persistent, pessimistic

Eccentric, inventive, rebellious, aloof

Empathetic, imaginative, escapist, unrealistic

Elements and Qualities

The twelve signs are divided into four elements, as well as three qualities. Each sign has its own unique pairing of element and quality, and understanding these combinations is helpful in understanding each sign and its role in the wheel.

ELEMENTS

There are four elements at play in the astrological wheel: fire, earth, air, and water. The elements associated with the signs are as follows:

 FIRE: ARIES, LEO, SAGITTARIUS
Fire signs are generally associated with the spirit, creation, passion, and temperament.

 EARTH: TAURUS, VIRGO, CAPRICORN
Earth signs are generally associated with the body, materiality, groundedness, and loyalty.

 AIR: GEMINI, LIBRA, AQUARIUS
Air signs are generally associated with the mind, ideas, connection, and social structures.

 WATER: CANCER, SCORPIO, PISCES
Water signs are generally associated with the emotions, intimacy, mystery, and psychic intuition.

QUALITIES

There are three qualities in the astrological wheel that separate the signs, and each of these sets contains one sign of each element. The qualities describe the role of that sign within the narrative arc of the wheel and elemental set. They are as follows:

CARDINAL: ARIES, CANCER, LIBRA, CAPRICORN
Cardinal signs occur at the beginning of the calendar seasons. They are associated with action, leadership, and initiative.

FIXED: TAURUS, LEO, SCORPIO, AQUARIUS
Fixed signs occur at the middle of the calendar seasons. They are associated with process, endurance, and work.

MUTABLE: GEMINI, VIRGO, SAGITTARIUS, PISCES
Mutable signs occur at the end of the calendar seasons. They are associated with growth, adaptation, and completion.

What's in a Birth Chart?

Have you ever read the description for your sun sign and thought: That's not quite me? As it turns out, you are more than just your sun sign. The time and place you were born unlock an entire system of houses (see page 20) and planetary positions (see page 22)—known as your birth chart, or natal chart—that provide a more nuanced picture of your personal astrology. By diving into your birth chart and deciphering its messages, you can use this book as a divining tool to get in touch with hidden aspects of yourself.

Three significant data points to note in your birth chart are your sun, moon, and rising signs. Even if you go no further in this section decoding the rest of your birth chart, your sun, moon, and rising gives you three robust facets to explore and reflect upon.

You may already know your sun sign, which is determined by your birthday. If you want to find your moon and rising signs, it's simple: you'll need your exact birth time and location. There is a plethora of calculators online for you to use—just do a quick internet search for astrology birth chart and pick a site that looks good to you. Plug in your info, and voila: Now you can see your sun, moon, rising, and other planetary placements in your birth chart, which make up your astrological portrait.

YOUR SUN SIGN is the astrological season you were born in and is a major player in the way you see and experience the world and relationships. Your sun sign influences your dominant personality, identity, and ego.

YOUR MOON SIGN, the sign the moon was in when you were born, represents your shadow self, the side not everyone sees—your home life, emotions, and relationships. Your moon sign also reveals how you deal with crisis and your instinctive coping mechanisms. See page 18 for more on the moon and its phases.

YOUR RISING (OR ASCENDANT) SIGN, the sign that was rising on the eastern horizon at the time and place of your birth, is the way you appear to the world: your look, your vibe, your voice. Your rising sign also determines the positions of your astrological houses, and acts as your first house, which we'll get into on page 20.

THE MOON

Following the eight phases of the moon is one way to use the astrological guidance in this book. Moon phases repeat roughly every 29.5 days, which gives you regular opportunities to check in with your own natural cycles of waxing and waning. Very generally, the waxing period from New Moon to Full Moon is good for manifesting, and the waning period from Full Moon to New Moon is good for banishing.

For each of the signs, we have provided a set of moon phase horoscopes. You may read them for your sun sign, your moon sign, the current astrological season, and/or the current moon sign.

MOON PHASE		AKA	KEYWORDS
	NEW MOON	Moon of Darkness	rest, recuperation, beginnings
	WAXING CRESCENT	Moon of Rebirth	energy, initiative, activation
	FIRST QUARTER	Moon of Momentum	balance, focus, commitment
	WAXING GIBBOUS	Moon of Gestation	patience, cultivation, fine-tuning

MOON FACTS!

- If your sun and moon are in the same sign, you were born on or near a new moon.

- If your sun and moon are in opposite signs, you were born on or near a full moon.

- Knowing what moon phase you are born on or near gives you an additional lens for considering what natural states you are drawn to in your inner life.

MOON PHASE		AKA	KEYWORDS
	FULL MOON	Moon of Celebration	completion, fulfillment, abundance
	WANING GIBBOUS	Moon of Dissemination	review, reflection, introspection
	LAST QUARTER	Moon of Retribution	discarding, amends, adjustment
	WANING CRESCENT	Moon of Harvest	transition, healing, closure

THE HOUSES

The astrological houses are twelve segments of the wheel that represent different facets of your life, and they form the foundational layer of your birth chart. The first house represents the self, and from there to the twelfth house, you travel in a narrative arc through the various sectors of your existence (such as your values, health, or career) and its relation to 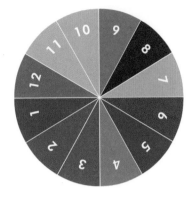 the world. Your houses are determined by your rising sign, which also determines the first house of your birth chart; your second through twelfth houses fall in succession after that around the wheel. We use the Whole Sign Houses astrological framework, which aligns each one of your houses with a unique sign in the wheel—that is, everyone has every sign in their chart, and they all have something to teach you according to where they fall.

The table below gives an overview of the houses and their associations. Each house also has a natural governing sign, but unless your rising sign is Aries, the sign positions in your chart will be different. One exercise is to note the contrasts between your houses' signs and the natural governing signs, and to try to intuit what the contrast might mean. You can use the houses as a lens by which to read the horoscopes of various signs in this book. For example, if your fourth house is in Libra, you might read the Libra horoscopes through the lens of home and family; if your seventh house is in Taurus, you may read the Taurus horoscopes under the lens of partnerships and relationships.

HOUSE	HOUSE OF	KEYWORDS
FIRST HOUSE	Self	First impressions, appearance, identity, ego, beginnings (Note: This is the house of your rising sign)
SECOND HOUSE	Value	Possessions, money, self-worth, substance, growth
THIRD HOUSE	Connection	Communication, transportation, information, intellect, technology
FOURTH HOUSE	Foundation	Home, family, ancestry, security, privacy
FIFTH HOUSE	Expression	Creativity, romance, play, passion, will, character
SIXTH HOUSE	Function	Health, service, routine, skills, craft, caretaking
SEVENTH HOUSE	Relation	Partnerships, collaboration, agreements, diplomacy, attraction
EIGHTH HOUSE	Transformation	Death and rebirth, sexuality, mystery, karma, taboos
NINTH HOUSE	Exploration	Journeys, adventure, knowledge, philosophy, culture, ethics
TENTH HOUSE	Ambition	Career, status, motivation, structure, authority, public image
ELEVENTH HOUSE	Humanity	Society, collectives, originality, innovation, social justice, hope, the future
TWELFTH HOUSE	Spirituality	Endings, the afterlife, imagination, dreams, the subconscious

THE PLANETS

When you were born, the sun, moon, and planets were all acrobating around different points in the universe. The exact placements of the planets when you entered the world make up the second layer of your birth chart, overlaid on top your house wheel.

Each of the planets (including the sun and moon, which astrologically serve as planets) represent basic unconscious energies in our psyches, which manifest as needs and drives. The sun, moon, Mercury, Venus, and Mars determine personal energies. Jupiter and Saturn determine social energies, which you'll share with people of a similar age group. Uranus, Neptune, and Pluto determine collective energies, which you'll share with people of the same generation. Each of the planets also rules at least one of the twelve signs, which brings us full circle in the associations between signs, houses, and planets.

The chart below gives you some general traits associated with each of the planets and the signs they rule over—see if you can cross-reference planets to signs and see their correlations. Looking at which signs and houses your planets are positioned in can help you understand how those energies are expressed. Based on which houses your planets live in, some signs may have a stronger pull than others, and indicate areas where you may focus or struggle. And houses empty of planets do not indicate a lack—these are places where you may find ease, insight, and tools for navigating your more active houses.

To give you an example of how planets, signs, and houses work together, let's say you have Venus in Scorpio, in your Fourth House. Venus is associated with how you deal with and express love and attraction, and Scorpio is a sign that is mysterious, intense, and turbulent, so a Venus in Scorpio would mean your romantic side takes on these and other attributes of Scorpio. Because your Venus in Scorpio is in your Fourth House, and the Fourth House is associated with the home, your romantic self may manifest through domestic or familial means.

	PLANETS	STATEMENT	KEYWORDS	RULES
☉	SUN	I am	dominant personality, identity	Leo
☽	MOON	I feel	emotions, inner life, home	Cancer
☿	MERCURY	I think	mind, ideas, communication	Gemini, Virgo
♀	VENUS	I love	value, attraction, relation	Taurus, Libra
♂	MARS	I act	drive, energy, confidence	Aries
♃	JUPITER	I grow	luck, wisdom, expansion	Sagittarius
♄	SATURN	I achieve	discipline, fears, challenges	Capricorn
♅	URANUS	I evolve	change, originality, discovery	Aquarius
♆	NEPTUNE	I dream	healing, imagination, escape	Pisces
♇	PLUTO	I empower	upheaval, rebirth transformation	Scorpio

Deciphering Your Birth Chart

Translating your birth chart's secret messages doesn't need to be a complicated endeavor—think of it like a mystical mad libs. We've provided some simple formulas below to get you started. We've also included an example of a birth chart that we've begun to break down for you, and we invite you to finish the exercise and make some of your own interpretations by referring back to the tables on the previous pages.

SUN / MOON / RISING

Formula:

This person's _____ comes across as _____ .

aspect of self · sign characteristic

Looking at this chart, we can infer that this person is:

- Sun in Capricorn (5th House): This person's dominant personality is one that is serious and ambitious, and these qualities manifest greatly in their creativity and self-expression.

- Moon in Cancer (11th House): This person's inner life is sensitive and protected, and these qualities impact the way they consider like-minded groups and the future.

- Since Capricorn and Cancer are opposite signs, you can infer that this person was born on or near a full moon.

- Virgo Rising (1st House): This person's first impression and appearance come across to others as meticulous and reserved.

Birth chart for person born on January 7, 2012, 8:23 PM in New York, NY

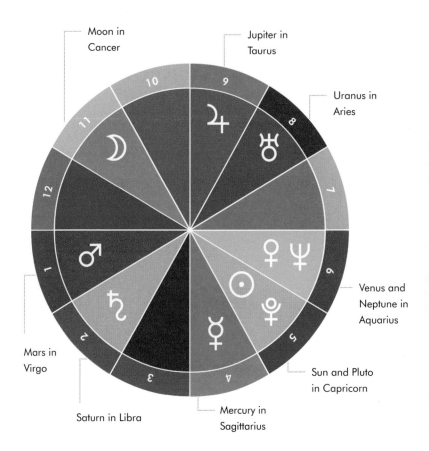

Moon in Cancer

Jupiter in Taurus

Uranus in Aries

Venus and Neptune in Aquarius

Sun and Pluto in Capricorn

Mercury in Sagittarius

Saturn in Libra

Mars in Virgo

PLANET IN SIGN / HOUSE

Formula:

This person's _____ expresses itself as _____
                planet   sign
       characteristic   characteristic

and is generally manifested in their _____ area of life.
                                              house
                                      characteristic

When it comes to the other planets and houses, this person has:

- Mars in Virgo (1st House): This person's drive and energy is expressed as meticulous and reserved, and it manifests in their core identity.

- Saturn in Libra (2nd House): This person is disciplined about or is challenged by diplomacy and balance, and it particularly impacts their values and concepts of worth.

- Mercury in Sagittarius (4th House): This person actively thinks about seeking adventure and knowledge, and it particularly impacts how they consider the home and family.

As practice, see if you can intuit the meanings of the rest of this person's chart, referencing the formulas we've given you. As you gain experience in reading these chart details, you'll be able to layer in additional meanings and deepen your understanding of how they interact. You can always reference these tables for the basics, and the signs' chapters for more nuance.

How to Use This Book

Now that you have the basics down, you can dive into the next section, the grimoire itself. We have divided it up by the signs, and each one comes with sets of horoscopes by moon phase and mood, suggestions for creating altars, seasonal affirmations, and creative rituals. They are designed to be evergreen and can be revisited as you see fit. As this section has demonstrated, you can use every chapter, not just your sun sign.

Here are the many ways you can use this book:

- Get to know your sun, moon, and rising signs

- Use the book as a calendar, starting with the current astrological season and working your way through

- Use the book according to the current moon phase and sign

- Use the book in the order of your house positions, working your way through your birth chart

- Using the attributes of the houses and your planetary positions, consult the signs about specific questions and life events

- Read the charts of your friends, family, acquaintances, and strangers

- Hop around! Mix and match! Create your own systems and interpretations!

Fill out a chart for someone you love!

NAME: BIRTH TIME: BIRTH LOCATION:

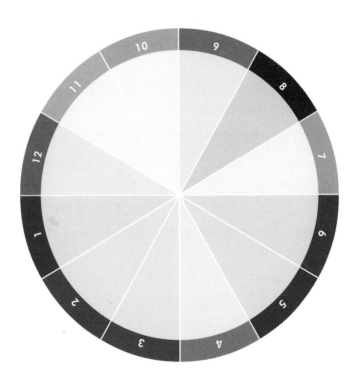

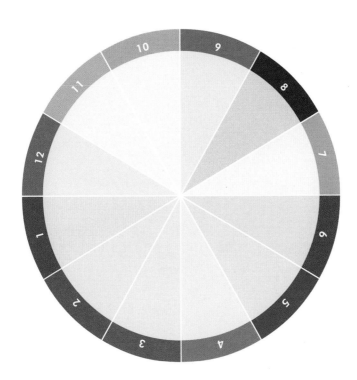

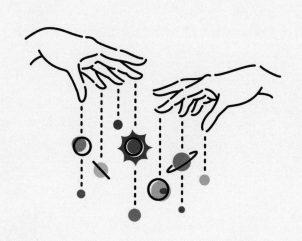

THE
SIGNS

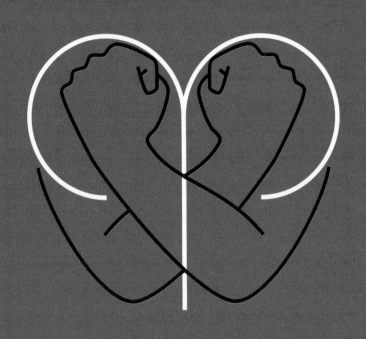

Aries

MARCH 21—APRIL 20
First House of Self

This is a time to be a rule-breaking, restless spirit. There is no box that can contain you—you can mold it to your shape through sheer force of will. That confidence is a flame that can draw others near you like moths buzzing around a street lamp to try to get close to all that passion. This is a time when nonconformity might only fuel your restlessness and drive to be different, to be first, to be best. The people who know how to handle you know how to give you the space you need to grow into all the different versions of yourself you will become. Change is in this part of your hardwiring, and destruction can only come at your own hands, not the hands of others. You are not easily damaged or broken. Often, however, you will need to bang up your own head and heart a few times rather than heed the cautionary tales of others—you're all leaping and zero looking. This fury and spark can ruin relationships as much as it can serve as radiant inspiration to others. You can exist purely as you are, flaws blazing, yet this is a time that can sometimes prevent you from the self-reflection you so desperately need.

CONSTELLATION
The Ram

ELEMENT
Fire

RULING PLANET
Mars

QUALITY
Cardinal

Moon Phase Horoscopes

NEW MOON *rest, recuperation, beginnings*

WAXING CRESCENT *energy, initiative, activation*

Close your eyes and listen to the thumping: Your own tiny, beating universe that you travel through also needs to slow down on its axis. This blood rushing through your ears might agitate you, but listen instead for its invitation to think before you react. Before you make a decision, look outside and see if you can name all the blues in the sky. What message would you write to yourself on the blank slate of a cloud if you could? Paying attention to the sensory information around you can slow your pounding heart down just long enough to make a better decision. Listen to music with no words; listen to distant bird songs and dog howls; listen for what the blank sounds between notes have to tell you.

Resist the urge to leap over the gate, blazing in all directions. The time for that will come, but now is for preparing for what's to come next and donning the armor you'll need to endure the things you haven't thought of yet. Sink into the molten core of yourself. Let yourself inhabit this space that can forge the next version of you; let yourself become sharpened and glinting, gathering all your powers. When you expand, the universe will meet you at the edge. The effort you put into being ready to greet it will enable you to listen instead of react. Make a list of everything you're going to need in order to be ready, assign each item a song, and play them every day to remind yourself of the path ahead.

FIRST QUARTER *balance, focus, commitment*

If you stay real still, you might notice that your veins are coursing with a wild and unfamiliar energy. It can be hard to know how to harness it—sometimes it's easier to let it distract you than to realize the precise power you have over your own life. It might startle you or even scare you. Just try to believe in your own strange magic, even when your own shaky thoughts are still taking shape. Try not to doubt what they can do. The universe tests you when it wants to see what you're made of and what you can really do. Look at videos of liquid light shows or quasars colliding. What would they look like inside you? What kinds of magic would they produce? List the things waiting to be born.

WAXING GIBBOUS *patience, cultivation, fine-tuning*

Even at the swift gallop with which you move, you can see the horizon stretch out in front of you. But staring into the future can make you trip over your present. If you feel impatient to get there, try to focus on the small things that pass you by, like murmurs on the bus or blades of grass. Noticing these small points in your day means moving more slowly through the world. When you look at the night sky, see how slowly the stars move across the sky. Think of how long it took them to get there, to burst into luminous brilliance. Remember that you have this same slow becoming in you. Pick a constellation and study its history and mythology. Then write your own and connect the dots. What is the next dot?

FULL MOON *completion, fulfillment, abundance*

WANING GIBBOUS *review, reflection, introspection*

Pay attention to the patterns and tiny synchronicities all around you: words you hear repeated, songs that come on the radio right after you think of them. What is the world trying to tell you about this moment, about where you are right now? What is pushing through to be noticed? Think of all these different shining blips of your day as jigsaw puzzle pieces. What if they are the answers to questions you haven't asked yet? During this time, keep a list of the textures that pass through your day, the ones that glimmer and ask to be noticed: songs, words, colors, smells. Then step back and look at them on the page. How do they fit together? Think of these coincidences as secret codes meant just for you, patiently waiting to be solved.

You might feel the shape of your own life start to vibrate and shift. Let this happen. By giving in to change, the truth of who you are will stay solid and real at its molten core. You won't desert yourself as long as you keep holding hands with that center. Watching the way things transition and shift on a larger scale can help you: Go outside when you wake up and watch the sky turn pink and the afternoon clouds effortlessly change shape as they were born to do. Sometimes you must turn your gaze outward to be inspired and reassured. Take a glass of water and mix in a drop of color. Keep adding drops of new colors and watch them shift and change. Think about what wants to shift inside you and about what color it is becoming.

LAST QUARTER *discarding, amends, adjustment*

WANING CRESCENT *transition, healing, closure*

You might have the unsettling sensation that nobody really sees you sometimes, that nobody knows who you really are. It might feel truly lonely, as if you're too bright and sharp for the world you're living in. But what these moments usually catch are times when you're changing and shifting, times when the new parts of you have yet to be named, so the old parts feel brittle and exposed. Spend a while befriending them and getting to know them; thank them for all that they've done for you. Write them a thank-you letter, reminiscing about all the times they protected you, and then bury or burn it. Wait to see what shows up in their place. This discarding of old selves can feel a little unsettling. Fill yourself up with art, music, and poetry.

Your powers can grow exponentially in proportion to the heat in your blood and the fire in your eyes. It's okay to get loud, to get firm, to draw lines in the sand. Tap into the energy in your beating heart and the twitchiness of your fingers. Look for your reflection in windows, puddles, and mirrors. See what it is trying to tell you when you're caught off guard by it. Your eyes might have a message about what you're hungry for; your hair might point you in a new direction. Write a list of all the things you started during this cycle, from the smallest to the biggest. Cross off the things you finished. What is remaining that you want to take with you? What is ready to grow during the next cycle? What can you leave behind? Lean into the growing pains.

Mood Phase Horoscopes

ROMANCE

Sometimes we get so wrapped up in telling ourselves who we think we are that we forget about the muscles we don't use. The person who gets you can intuit when you need to let your flame turn down to a soft blue. And they know when you're trying to ram your horns through walls when you could just walk through the door instead. In order for you to expand to your full size, you need to be reminded that you're not always right, and that that's okay. Your challenge is to sometimes take off your blinders—the ones that keep your gaze so sharply focused on the future. Practice trusting the people you love to sometimes show you a different path.

REFLECTION

Reflecting requires a rearview mirror, and yours is probably gathering dust somewhere. Why look backward at what has already transpired? But there is benefit to be gained in taking a beat to slow down and think about the past. You can learn from your missteps, for one. Or take stock of lessons learned. As much as you might not want to believe it, we're all creatures of habit, and progress isn't as linear and straightforward as you'd like to believe. While it's important not to dwell (something no one would accuse you of anyway), finding the equation of your patterns can be useful if you find yourself in the same fiery pit again or backed into a familiar corner on occasion.

ANGER

Anger is almost always a cover for something boiling away underneath: shame, disappointment, hurt, or powerlessness. When you don't take the time to peer below the surface, you risk repeating the same situations that trigger your anger. You need to remove yourself from the source of the heat in order to gain clarity. The downside of intensity is not giving yourself the time to move through all the shades that come before and after—you just want to get through as quickly as possible. Look up all the shades of red that exist in the world. Read them; see them. Spend time being each one, from the palest simmer to the brightest scream. Spend time in the ones that feel foreign and that slow you down enough to think.

CONNECTION

Fear is often a mask for something much more granular that we are worried about. A way to make your friendships stronger is to find common ground in your vulnerabilities, as hard as that may be. And once you witness someone's secrets and fears, you need to treat those thoughts like the delicate jewels they are. It's very easy for you to make friends but be careful not to inadvertently create distance by blazing hot and strong only to forget about the bond you forged in the next moment. People are softer than you think. Even though this part of you prides itself on saying exactly what you feel and think rather than keeping it bottled up, remember to allow people the space to process your emotional output.

 ## ACTION

Who are you when you take it slow? Sometimes we believe things are so constitutionally a part of our nature that we have a hard time remembering that we know any other way. Sometimes it's that we associate an action with a feeling, such as that taking your time means getting bored. But sometimes blazing ahead without thinking about it means you lack the insight to know why it is you're doing what you're doing. Insight is the only way you can grow, or keep from repeating past mistakes. You'd prefer to grow by constantly challenging your limits, and that's okay too. But just as you pride yourself in flexing those muscles, it's necessary to try out the weaker ones and see how they work as well.

STRENGTH

Strength is a stone with many facets—emotional, physical, and spiritual. While the different parts of you have different strengths, there's an aspect of you that can handle a great deal on all counts—almost as though it were forged into your very constitution. Something that might surprise you is the notion that vulnerability is also one facet on this stone. This is because it requires a different kind of bravery to be vulnerable and to let it be seen by others. But the truth is that showing it is the secret glue that can bond you to others, that can create mutual trust. Although you might prefer others to see you as indestructible and unbreakable, that doesn't create a mutuality by which others can relate to and therefore respect you.

 **STAGNATION**

Uncertainty can make you behave like a bull in a china shop, provoking everyone into reacting. People are more sensitive to this energy than you'd imagine, and your restlessness can be contagious—dredging up the very energy you're trying to dispel. This might be because it's easy to conflate indecision with boredom, something this part of you can become deeply allergic to. Part of this frustration can stem from the fact that you are fundamentally aware that you create your own sense of happiness. In these in-between spaces, practice the art of channeling your indecision into something physical and concrete: Go for a run, paint a picture using all the red paints you own, or build an intricate birdhouse.

WORK

Stamina is something this part of you has in spades, yet when combined with serial restlessness, it can mean that you grow bored easily. One thing that can bog you down in the quicksand is being forced to go over tedious details rather than paint your ideas in broad, excited strokes. The best environment for you to thrive is one in which you are given autonomy. Anything that caters to stimulation and excitement will hold your attention, or anything that requires you to travel, move, and create things that didn't exist before. A challenge is the ability to truly listen to the advice from those who have your best interest at heart, though they might have to trick you into believing you're breaking the rules.

Altar

This season, use your altar as a launchpad for new beginnings.

Decorate your altar with loud reds, invoking fire and sparks.

Call upon the ram and other assertive, hot-tempered creatures.

Place offerings of matches and fire starters, hot peppers, spicy scents, and things and images you associate closely with your identity and presentation.

Charge your altar with a bold declaration of your existence.

Affirmations

I make myself available to receiving my calling.

I am the strongest when I commit to living my truth.

I choose to ride the energy of the momentum I harness.

I release the ego that leads me astray.

Rituals

IMPULSE VS. INTUITION

Think of a decision you are trying to make—perhaps it's something you feel conflicted about or a situation in which you are trying not to repeat old, tired habits. Make a list below: write down every quick impulse that comes to mind about your decision. Then, take a deep breath. To the right of each item, write how each impulse makes you feel. Pay attention to your heart. Is it speeding up? Now close your eyes and take a deep breath. Pretend your brain is a radio, and scan through the channels and chatter until you hear silence. Ask the silence: What should I do? Wait patiently until the silence answers.

_____

_____

_____

_____

_____

_____

_____

_____

_____

_____

_____

INNER BEAST

Position yourself in front of a mirror so that your face is visible. Conjure up something that is most infuriating to you and let it fill your body with the kind of white-hot rage that makes you want to smash windows. Channel that energy into your face and let it warp your features into an image of formidable terror. Do not shy away from the folds, creases, exposed gums, furrowed brows, bloodthirsty pupils, and dripping saliva. Let this image of your face sear itself into your heart. This is your inner beast. It has your back, but be careful not to relinquish too much of your power to it. Draw your inner beast below.

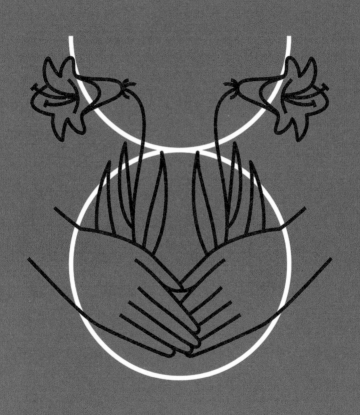

Taurus

APRIL 20—MAY 21
Second House of Value

What does it mean to be more solid than a tree? This part of you is made of roots that seek out the dirt or a slow furnace that emits a steady heat. It's that warmth and rootedness that pulls those who are seeking shelter and safety toward you. If you were a house, every room would be filled with soft blankets, fresh flowers, and home-baked bread. Your five senses are how you experience and interact with the world. Yet this same seeking of what's solid can knock you off kilter when you're confronted by change, choice, or natural chaos. The same qualities that grace this part of you with tenderness and practicality can provoke in you an inflexibility and tendency to stagnate.

CONSTELLATION
The Bull

ELEMENT
Earth

RULING PLANET
Venus

QUALITY
Fixed

The truth you will have to face in this life is that it isn't always harmonious, and if you don't learn to bend to life's disorder, inflexibility can grind you down. How can you learn to embrace the fact that life, and people, are constantly changing? Your secret power is that you know your own center. During times of uncertainty that threaten to topple you, you can bring the same nurturing and compassion you give to those you love to yourself.

Moon Phase Horoscopes

NEW MOON *rest, recuperation, beginnings*

Who are you when you're not trying to keep yourself solid and upright? Sometimes it's okay to go soft around the edges, to shake off the dirt from your roots, and to see what it feels like to let go of certainty. Now is the time to get still and check your own beating heart and the shape of the clouds that are flitting across your mind. Practice lying down where you can see out the window and studying the way stillness deepens in between the chirping of birds and the hum of cars. Imagine living in that stillness, just for a minute. What acceptance can you find there? This is a time for resting your heart, a time for listening to its sigh. What does it sound like? Listen to songs with no words and write or draw whatever comes into your mind.

WAXING CRESCENT *energy, initiative, activation*

It might feel as if you're emerging from a long hibernation or a weird boring loop. You might feel overwhelmed by all the potential paths stretching out into the horizon, all the future versions of you that already exist. It might make you too scared to move. Just keep your gaze soft and focused. Stay open to every eerie possibility and every disguised gift. Imagine you're a seed ready to be watered. What will make you grow and bend toward the light? Keep a plant on your windowsill. Notice how its leaves turn toward the direction the light comes in. How can you angle yourself the same way in order to grow toward the life you want? It requires knowing what those possible lives look like, so draw them and write love letters to them.

FIRST QUARTER *balance, focus, commitment*

WAXING GIBBOUS *patience, cultivation, fine-tuning*

Now is the time to tap into the part of you that is famous for its rooting tendencies. The upside to strength is a tendency toward unwavering calm and resolute braveness. This means that now is the time to take risks, to move in a direction you have yet to grow. There's a lesson for you in this unfurling. It takes time, but it honors slowness and steadiness. And it's a time to keep your eyes on the next few steps rather than the distant horizon. Remember that if you get knocked off balance, you can always find your way back to yourself. Move your body in ways that require strength. Practice standing on one leg until it gets tired, until you waver and need to rest and find your center again. Memorize this feeling. It is always available to you.

This is truly your time to shine, to dig in deep and put your famous patience and plodding tenacious-ness to work. People tend to underestimate you because you make hard work look easy, but the truth is that you know how to be your own support system. You are by turns the soil, the roots, the leaves, and the sun. Don't fool yourself into believing that you don't already have the pieces of the life you want to build, that you don't already contain everything you need. Go outside and find a stone. Put it in a place where you can see it, all solid and true and patient in its stone-ness. Add a new stone every day until you've built something solid and true for yourself as well. What other form-less ideas need firm structures that you can build?

FULL MOON *completion, fulfillment, abundance*

WANING GIBBOUS *review, reflection, introspection*

Pay attention to the sounds and ideas that want to come out of you in the same way that you listen to the wind, trees, and birds outside your window. Notice all the new colors emerging; notice all the quiet joy hiding around you. Write your finds in a notebook; color them in or record their sounds. The same fertility and aliveness you notice around you lives in you, too, and can always be activated through your senses. Now is the time for immersing yourself in long baths or for getting a full night's sleep and writing down the sensations from your dreams when you wake up. Are they different from the senses you feel in waking life? What do they want you to pay attention to?

It can be hard for you to let go— of things, of people, of places. Holding on can be good sometimes; it's what gives you endurance for the long haul of this expansive life you're living. But the risk you run if you can't put things down once they're done is that you'll get stuck there. You might trick yourself into believing you're just being patient, or devoted, or true. But you know how the heaviness sinks into your bones, has you glancing backward instead of gazing at the horizon. Write a list of the things in your life that are finished but that still occupy your consciousness. Hold each one in your mind and reassure it that by putting it down you won't be forgetting it but, rather, setting it free with gratitude.

LAST QUARTER *discarding, amends, adjustment*

We have equilibrium for only so long until the living of life sloshes the water out of our perfectly level aquarium bowl. People and places staying the same are reassuring to you, but you also have a deep appreciation for the way things change in their own sweet time in nature. Tap into the awe you have for these ebbs and flows and hold the same reverence for your own tides. Find a patch of nature and get close to the ground. Notice how some things have decayed while other things are about to bloom. What attachments can you compost that are no longer useful? Remember that some things must go to make space for the things that have waited so patiently for you to be ready.

WANING CRESCENT *transition, healing, closure*

Think about the feeling you get when you've reached the top of a mountain. You stop for a moment to catch your breath, feel the sweat dry on your skin, take in what you've left in the distance below. You know you have to go back down eventually, but you also know everything will look a little different, a little more vibrant and knowing—as if the world knows you conquered something. Slow and steady has never let you down, even when others race past you in anticipation to get to the same place you'll get to eventually. From this vantage point, you're also able to see that you already have the answers you've been searching for, even though you've been stuck on the questions forever.

Mood Phase Horoscopes

 **ROMANCE**

There's a part of you that loves to be a solid, quiet force, and there's no greater blanketing force than love. Yet you also know that love is never a sure thing. There's a sweet relief in certainty, but by being cautious, you miss out on the fluttering in-betweens, the swirling dust that gets kicked up between two people while they lose their balance and fall deep down in it. Consider the notion that this desire to possess something as ineffable as a person comes from a yearning to control the past, present, or future—all of which only operate if you accept both their fixed and fluid natures. Practice sinking in the rooted, bottomless softness of your own being, which knows exactly what you need and where to find it.

 **SUFFERING**

The problem with being such a sturdy source for others is that they might never suspect the depths of sadness. It's one thing to present a serene front, but it's another thing to allow someone to glimpse the sticky sap that lies underneath. The irony is that in order to feel known you must let others into the wobbly parts of you, which are really the parts yearning to be noticed. Try to tap into your intuition that this is just one ripple in the cycles of life and that you will always expand outward again. When you find yourself becoming listless, call a friend with whom you can just quietly exist. Remind yourself that other people like to be needed, too, and that being needed by you is a deep honor.

STAGNATION

What looks like indecision is often just quiet and intense internal deliberation. Your clock ticks a few beats slower than everyone else's, and that's not only okay but also it often is an advantage. The challenge you can run into is that rarely is anything a sure thing, and waiting for a sign that it is means a greater possibility that it will pass you by. Remember to allow yourself some time to unfold your feelings without feeling rushed. If you find yourself gripped by inertia, try taking one small action toward a decision—write a list, go for a walk, stare out the window and think. Remind yourself of all the good and true and sure decisions you've made before and how sharp it has calibrated your internal compass.

REFLECTION

There's a part of you that is so clear in its visions and necessities for living this one true life of yours. Because you have this clarity, you can tap into the messages that nudge you slyly in the direction you need to move. It pays to ask yourself what rhythm of life you currently inhabit. Rather than thinking or feeling, your point of access is through your senses, which inform your deeper intuitions. Breathe in the air around you; dig your fingers into the ever-evolving soil; taste the fears that sneak into the back of your throat. This part of you knows what to keep and what must go. Your secret talent is the ability to catch hold of these dreams and to nurture them into existence with patience.

 **CHANGE**

Outwardly, being truly stuck can look a lot like you when you're in motion. This is because this part of you is slow and deliberate; it takes it's time to calculate the geometry of facts and intuition that can help you make the right decision. But there's a difference between thinking and existing, between weighing your options and becoming paralyzed by them. One way to intuit the difference is to notice how they feel in your body: True stuckness is a sludgy lifelessness, a turning inward out of avoidance. Take the time to check in with each twitchy muscle, each firing nerve. Your body has messages for you to deliver to your mind. What does it want to say? How can it help you get unstuck?

 **CONNECTION**

There's a part of you that comes truly alive when nurturing the people you love, providing the pure currency of blankets and toast. It's that connection with the physical world that allows you to see how people are compassionately connected. There's a patient and stable quality to you that attracts people looking for a sense of home, of unyielding support. Remember, though, that not everyone expresses support in the same way, and it can be easy for you to feel as if you're not getting as good as you're giving. The next time you're with a friend, practice being completely present with who they are in this moment, remembering that we are all mercurial beings with ever-shifting needs, moods, and experiences. Accept people on their terms, not just yours.

WORK

The way you approach the world through your work shapes your identity as a creator, a communicator, and a collaborator. This is a part of you that relishes shaking the foundation of what you are creating until you know it is going to stand the stress of whatever you pile on top of it. The quality that lends itself to this kind of endeavor is tenaciousness, a fixed ability to let things take the time they're going to take without being rushed. Practice the art of visioning all the stages of a process, of feeling what it will be like to fully inhabit each step. Keep plants around you so you can be reminded of what it means for something to take root and unravel on its own time.

ANGER

Think of a murmuring bee, all indolent sweetness, taking its time to choose the right flower. But swat a bee or upset its equilibrium and notice its buzz grow indignant, its movements becoming jagged and sharp. The heat of your anger tends to surprise others who have only glimpsed your stubbornness through the lens of your loyalty. The next time you feel this buzzing heat your veins, ask yourself what flame has lit it. Anger is merely an outward reaction to whatever it is that is really bothering you. Try to keep from going rigid and fixed, and instead try to access the soft, steady part of you that knows how to calm, soothe, and nurture not only others but also yourself.

Altar

This season, use your altar as a temple to self-worth and gratitude.

Decorate your altar with lush greens and florals, invoking the sensual earth.

Call upon the bull and other gentle, sturdy, stubborn beasts.

Place offerings of bread and baked goods, savory herbs, houseplants, fresh flowers, personal treasures, coins, flower essences, and oils.

Finish your altar by presenting a small token of appreciation to yourself, in any form.

Affirmations

I determine the rules for my own value system.

I open myself to the resources that will help me build what I need.

I sow the seeds for the blossoms that will come.

I am worthy, I am significant, I am enough.

Rituals

LETTING GO

Think of something you can't let go of: an old belief, a person, a relationship, a place. Write a letter to that thing or person detailing all the reasons you can't give it up. What has it done for you? What have you learned from it? What do you want to say to it that you weren't able to when you wanted to? Now tell it why you need to say goodbye. Even if it hurt you or haunts you, thank it for its lessons, but tell it why you no longer need it.

_____

_____

_____

_____

_____

_____

_____

_____

_____

_____

_____

FLORAMANCY

Set aside twenty to sixty minutes to take a walk with no particular destination or end point. You can do this walk any time of year when plants and flowers grow outside. It's a good walk to do seasonally, to see how you've changed and the world has changed. How things leave and come back. Your goal on this walk is to look for different kinds of flowers or plants to pick, the ones that call to you or catch your eye. Slow down and really look. Let the flowers that call your attention guide the path of your walk. Keep picking and arranging them in your hand, seeing what different ones look like side by side, noticing their colors and textures. After you feel satiated, take your flowers home and put them in water where you can see them. Think about why you were drawn to their colors and shapes, draw them below, and then write your associations. What do they want to tell you?

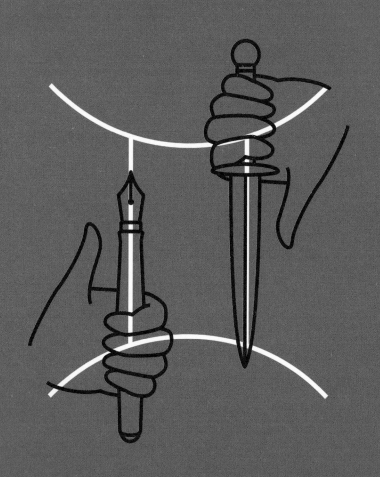

Gemini

Third House of Connection

Nobody ever knows what they're gonna get with this part of you. Here lies two for the price of one, represented by the Twins, and you can be the embodiment of this duality down to your very core. This means you're host to many varied moods—sometimes all in the same breath: serious and moody, outgoing and shy, charming and brooding. But this ability to shift so quickly from one gear to the next can make you adaptable in a way that sparks and inspires both yourself and others. Because your mind is usually going a mile a minute, you're usually the most interesting person to talk to at a party, where you can dazzle everyone with your wit while also retaining an air of intriguing moodiness. There's a sense of never knowing what's coming next in your presence, for better or for worse. You're definitely the sign most likely to host and ghost your own party. Yet, this part of you doesn't mind being alone—it can help generate all your weirdest ideas. Embrace this curiosity, which gives you the ability to digest a wide variety of influences quickly and spit out your own wild creations in response.

CONSTELLATION
The Twins

ELEMENT
Air

RULING PLANET
Mercury

QUALITY
Mutable

Moon Phase Horoscopes

NEW MOON *rest, recuperation, beginnings*

Let yourself soften around the edges for a minute; let your eyes lose focus and your mind grow wavy. What strange new shapes can you find there? What new weird sounds do you notice in the distance? This stillness can be hard for you, but sometimes it's necessary in order to regenerate. Sometimes you need to tune into a new frequency in order to recharge, re-stimulate. Don't let it make you feel too restless about what happens next. Just be open to wordless interpretation. Find an open window and stare at the still point of the horizon. It has things to tell you about yourself, things you can only hear if you get real quiet and tune in to the deep hum that lies past the voices chattering in your brain.

WAXING CRESCENT *energy, initiative, activation*

Sometimes you feel like a balloon that needs to be popped. It can feel itchy, like hearing a high-pitched sound no one else can. Pay attention, though. Something in you wants to break free and to unfurl its tentacles, and show you new ways to see. Like any new way of being, it might feel strange at first, like wearing glasses with a new prescription. Try focusing on the different sensory inputs in your life. Draw pictures of your dreams and write down the glimmers of life that shine bright for you right now: songs, conversations, faces. Study their strange, beautiful geometry. Listen to music with no words. Listen to music that sounds as if it were composed by extraterrestrials. What truths can you make out?

FIRST QUARTER *balance, focus, commitment*

WAXING GIBBOUS *patience, cultivation, fine-tuning*

This is a part of you that is so good at ideas. You've got all the ideas in the world, and often you get sidelined by the fact that no one can read your mind to keep up with you. It's easy to get excited by ideas, but how can you turn them into something real? Think about a whirling dervish gathering all that speed and dust until it's a force to be reckoned with. How can you find a place to touch down, to bring to life the ideas flitting around your mind? Write your ideas down on small pieces of paper and put them in a bag. Pull one out. Think about what comes next in order for it to happen. Do it. Remember that these moments of pause are always available to you as a way to find clarity.

Slowing down is hard. Think of the stillness before a summer storm; think of the tightness of a bud before it blossoms. Ideas can't bloom without a necessary gestation. Details require patience and care, a deliberate tending-to. It can be easy to give up before the first growth pokes through. What if you knew you were almost there? Tie a piece of yarn into a complicated knot. Then unknot it. This is the focus that is required of you in order to bring what you want into the light of day. Listen to complicated piano pieces and imagine all the precise move-ments the fingers of the player must make. How can you work on precision and focus? If you get antsy, take a walk. Come back. Keep going.

FULL MOON *completion, fulfillment, abundance*

WANING GIBBOUS *review, reflection, introspection*

Look around you. What is presenting itself to you in abundance right now? It might show up in unusual shapes. You may not even be able to touch it, but if you pay attention, you can feel it. Press the mute button on your internal chatter and instead notice how this abundance makes you feel in your bones. How did you call it into existence? Your dreams might have something to tell you about what's lurking under the surface of your subconscious, trying to poke through for you to grab hold of and make real. Rather than let their shadows make you nervous, try to decipher the messages you're receiving. Draw pictures of the messages as people or blobs, and give them each a name. Check in with them next month.

Your own wild, unpredictable world that you travel through can feel calmer and kinder right now. Let the sharp voices in your head turn into gentle whispers, just for a minute. Know that if you can quiet the ones that take up the most space, you might hear the voices of new yous, voices only just beginning to gather strength and practice speaking. What old, tired ideas are you hanging onto too tightly? Imagine loosening your grip, for a moment, to see if they will stay put or float away. Sometimes you need to empty yourself out even if it makes you feel unsure. Dump out a drawer in your house. Sort all its odds and ends back into their homes. Throw away what doesn't fit. Apply this methodical task to yourself.

LAST QUARTER *discarding, amends, adjustment*

This part of you loves change, and now is a time to lean into whatever shifts are coming your way. What seeds have you sown; what is beginning to pop up out of your fertile mind, all tender? How can you give your thoughts the space to grow without forcing them? Things unfurl in their own sweet time, and the risk is getting bored before you can see them bloom. Buy a small plant, put it in some soil, give it some water, and walk away. Check back in a week and see what's unfurled in its own quiet, determined timeline. In order to make space, you'll need to check in with yourself to see what is ready to go. There's a reason farmers add soil every season—things can't continue to grow without it.

WANING CRESCENT *transition, healing, closure*

Think of the ways that your ideas have paid off in the past, and the bendy shapes they had to take to get there. The path from idea to action is rarely a straight line, but this part of you can easily embrace the unknowable twists and turns required. How can you get out of your own way? Go outside and pick a flower that has yet to blossom. Notice over the next few days how it grows new shoots and leaves whenever you aren't impatiently watching it. Write a poem about what it has to teach you about the silent mysteries of time and transition. How can you bend yourself toward the light, even if it means taking a less-traveled path? Think back toward the times in your life that you have branched out into new shapes.

Mood Phase Horoscopes

ROMANCE

If only you could hand out a detailed wheel chart of your moods according to the weather, time of day, or color of your pants. There's a part of you that's not even sure if you can explain you to yourself, let alone to other people. This tendency to change leads you to those who find your restless mind fascinating, not threatening. What you might crave most deeply, though, is someone to accept all your kaleidoscopic parts, all your selves, even the ones that seem contradictory. Remember that all your selves are valid, even if they change shape as often as light changes in a day. Seek out a muse rather than a rock, someone who sees you and encourages you to be whatever truth you're living in any moment.

REFLECTION

Thinking of beginnings, middles, and endings will get you nowhere, because this part of you experiences time as cyclical, spiral, and ever-contracting. Reflection can be an important ingredient in cultivating and getting real with yourself. Give yourself an hour to ride the bus and just stare out the window as the blur of trees whizzes by. Let your gaze go soft and let your thoughts drop off with the landscape. What feelings are directing the thoughts like neon arrows? Fill your notebook pages with strange spirals, weird geometries, temperamental colors. Label them with the different parts of your life, different feelings, different people. What patterns do you notice? What do the shapes have to tell you about yourself and about how the past, present, and future are connected?

CONNECTION

Think of moths and butterflies, flitting from light to light and flower to flower, drinking it all in and absorbing all that vibrancy and nourishment. Friendship for this part of you fulfills the same requirements—you can get so much of your energy and inspiration from others, delighting in the give-and-take, the unpredictability of moods and whims and urges. This can make you a buzzing excitement to be around, but it can also make you strangely hard to access on a deeper level. How can you remind yourself to stay present with people, to slow down long enough to let them access some of your interior layers? Find the people you connect with and water the connection by giving them your undivided attention.

 ## COMPASSION

There's a way that curiosity and compassion can bend and intersect, and this part of you uses your innate, sparking curiosity to learn about other people in the world in a way that generates an intellectual compassion. Since this part of you tends to experience the world through your intellect rather than your feelings, it lends you a reserve that allows you a radical suspension of judgment—a necessary component in true empathy. Remind yourself that this is a gift that gives you the ability to see the many-faceted and often conflicting sides of a person or situation, and therefore to see inherent, flawed, tender humanity. You can use this gift to grant the world your inventions, your excited ideas, and your wild solutions to loneliness and suffering.

 **STRENGTH**

One of the greatest strengths this part of you embodies is the ability to embrace and investigate your weaknesses as well. No other sign is perhaps so tuned into the nuances and spectrum of contradictions inherent in the notion of strengths and weakness. There's a deep realization that, oftentimes, one emerges or encourages the other, and this makes you ambidextrous in your ability to see the necessity of both. Think of the way that invisible reinforcements hold up towering skyscrapers. What are your secret skills of reinforcement? What stress tests can you perform to see how you hold up in moments of wavering doubt? Write a list of your strengths and weaknesses. Draw a line between the ones that support each other. Meditate on the ways they have served you.

STAGNATION

Imagine a large radio antenna on a distant planet, picking up every station in the universe. This is what this part of your brain feels like most days. In a way it can be invigorating: so many ideas and inspirations! Yet the downside is the hesitation to commit or to not lose steam once the commitment is made and the real work begins. Don't forget that you have a secret weapon: an authentic internal compass like nothing else, one that is constantly whispering which direction to take. Go in the direction of what makes you feel right in your bones. Picture the choices not in your mind but in your gut. Which one feels warmer? Which one feels colder? Always go with the one that gives the glow.

FEAR

Of all the many thoughts, feelings, and moods that flit through your consciousness, this part of you is able to handle fear, because your curious reserve allows you to analyze it rather than feel it. It equips you to move toward the things that scare you rather than away from them, and to exist within the different tensions that emerge when things aren't certain. Most people tend to take the shortest and clearest path to safety, but you're able to flip back and forth between different shimmering realities, even the ones that feel absolutely foreign. Use this gift to teach others how to sit with what might feel unbearable; show them the possibilities that leaning into fear can open up. Assigning reasons to your fears, rather than just reacting, can help you see them without their scary disguises.

 # SUFFERING

Even the people closest to you might be surprised to know how dark it can get in your brain. Where you can trap yourself is trying to think your way out of your feelings; then your thoughts can become weapons that turn against you. Rather than grasp for rational thoughts, allow yourself to sink into your feelings for a moment, as sharp and jagged as they might be. Then let your mind remember a time you felt this broken before. What feeling came after? And after that? Remember that your body and your brain are in a constant conversation. Think of a message your body has for your brain from the past, from a previous lesson about loss or sadness. Remember it and feel it in your bones.

Altar

This season, use your altar as a sounding board for your multi-faceted selves.

Decorate your altar with bright jolts of yellow, invoking the buzz of electricity.

Call upon the trickster archetypes and swift social creatures, such as bees or monkeys.

Place offerings of writing tools and stationery, crossword puzzles and brainteasers, words and images of transportation and communication.

Charge your altar by taking an intentional moment for deep awareness of your current surroundings.

Affirmations

I adapt to changing circumstances with openness and versatility.

I am capable of quick connections and keen insights.

I gather information from all sides before reaching conclusions.

I recognize the impact of language, so I choose my words wisely.

Rituals

NONDOMINANCE

This month, see if you can switch to your nondominant hand for one mundane daily activity. Maybe it is opening doors, brushing your teeth, or petting the cat. Notice how much more aware you are of exercising this muscle, both physically and psychologically. What are the things you are normally on autopilot about? What happens when you stop to shake up these automatic ways of being? Are you able to rewire yourself, or do you feel resistance? What can you learn?

INTEGRATING DUALITIES

This is a ritual to do when you are feeling torn between two selves, warring impulses, and conflicting thoughts. Take three different colors of string, ribbon, twine, or some other long and braidable material. Tie them together into a knot and pin them to the top of a piece of paper. On either side of the page, write down what each side or impulse wants to tell you. What do they want to say to each other? Notice any tensions that come up in your body as you write them down. Where are they located? Can you recognize the physical sensations as ones you have felt before? Take each thread between your fingers and braid them together while thinking of this question: Is there a middle path? What is it? Braid your string until you reach the ends and then tie it off in a tight knot. Keep a visual reminder of your middle path below.

Cancer

Fourth House of Foundation

You're a psychic sponge that feels every emotional note, and the half-notes too. Some artists paint with colors; you paint with feelings. The deep furry blues of sadness, or the white-hot strokes of joy. So much of the genesis for this rich palette is your sentimentality and your sensitivity to people and situations. This intuition draws others toward you with the magnetism of empathy and your tendency to nurture the ones you love. Your capacity for emotional depth is magnetic and reassuring, because it allows others the space to feel their feelings too. Even though you're a sponge, the way into the deepest rooms of your heart requires knowing when to leave you be with your feelings. Luckily for them, you don't mind being at home, building up some reserves of privacy and mystery. What some might read as initial aloofness is just a sincere desire for privacy in your protective shell. But the truth is also that you want so desperately to be known. No one can truly know you, though, unless you allow yourself to be seen, in all your glorious depths.

CONSTELLATION
The Crab

ELEMENT
Water

RULING PLANET
Moon

QUALITY
Cardinal

Moon Phase Horoscopes

NEW MOON *rest, recuperation, beginnings*

If there's one thing this part of you is good at it's sinking into your feelings. After marinating for awhile, though, it's good to let those feelings seep out of you in whatever way they need to: sometimes it's writing them down on scraps of paper and letting them blow off a windy hillside; sometimes it's mixing all the paint colors until you identify the combination that sets your feelings free. This might make you a little nervous. Remember that sometimes it's okay to be a blank canvas, ready to be filled with new colors of emotions. Sit somewhere you can see the clouds blow by. Assign each cloud a feeling you have that you can't shake. Then watch it change shape and disintegrate into the blue sky.

WAXING CRESCENT *energy, initiative, activation*

Who are you when nobody's watching? You're so good at taking care of the ones you love, but how do you take care of yourself? Do everything you can to remember how much and how deeply you are beholden only to you. It's only when you cement your own slow, steady, yearning path that you can show up fully for others without getting derailed. To do this, you need to give space to your own weird unspoken desires that you've been too scared to say out loud to yourself. Let them breathe; give them some water. Build a fort out of soft and sturdy objects in your home. Remember that you can carry this sense of security with you always, like a snail that carries its cozy, safe home with it wherever it goes.

FIRST QUARTER *balance, focus, commitment*

WAXING GIBBOUS *patience, cultivation, fine-tuning*

This is a time for choosing the wild unknown, as much and as often as you can. It can be hard to put a tentative claw out in the world, to test uncertain ideas. But it's the only way you're gonna expand. This is the only way to punch through what is holding you down. It's good to be on guard against the possibility that things might not turn out the way you want. But it's the only way to open yourself up to something more expansive. Focus on the spaces where your thoughts get unsure, the moments when your words get stuck in your throat. Sit with them and encourage them the same patient way you would with a friend. Draw or write them out and keep adding to them until they're crystal clear.

Try to tap into the weird and sad parts of yourself, all the things that make you get impatient and antsy, the things that make you snap and roll your eyes and retreat into your skin. In these small, forgotten moments, work to remember the gentleness buried in you. Remember to rehearse faith in your own abilities, in your own worthiness. Rehearse the feeling of the universe meeting you halfway, of finding out what happens when you say "Yes." The trick is that you can't rush it, and sometimes you have to sit with the itchiness. Make a list of all the ways you have been your own best friend. Try to have an imaginary phone call with your past selves and ask them for some gentle advice.

FULL MOON *completion, fulfillment, abundance*

The problem, little sponge, is that sometimes this part of you you absorbs more than you can handle, including other people's moods and feelings. Always remember that you are your own untapped source and that you have so much intuition stored inside you, like a weather vane in a lightning storm. It's okay to move as if you're underwater during the times when you're navigating which way to turn. It's okay if you don't yet know where all this dreaming will lead. Ask your wiser self to point which way to go in your dreams at night. Look for signs during the day that shimmer and vibrate—colors, songs, or strange cracks in the sidewalk. Be patient in demystifying their riddles and let them show you the way.

WANING GIBBOUS *review, reflection, introspection*

Go through your closets and peek under your bed. Scour all your old hiding places. Try to recall the things you've hidden from yourself, the things that you've promised you'll deal with later. These things are connected to old emotions— whole cupboards full of happiness and heartache—and you're going to want to cling to their stories. But first, you'll need to recall where you've locked them inside yourself. When you hold them up to the light, you might find that the things you thought were written in stone are now transparent. What stories do you tell about yourself that need to be rewritten to account for what's shifted in you? It's okay to hang out for a bit in the hollow space between who you were and who you're gonna be next.

LAST QUARTER *discarding, amends, adjustment*

It's a great time to chat with what's haunting you. Let the tears leak out of your eyes and then let them go. You tend to hold on to a lot—old friends, lovers, and memories that flit in and out like moths. Those things can be a way to see how you've arrived here in this moment. You might encounter new versions of these people and places that look different on the surface but are so, so familiar underneath their veneers. But you will be different. And in order to understand how, you'll need to be able to see clearly in the rearview mirror. Make a list of what you need to say goodbye to. Bury your list in a place that you can visit when you need to. Thank the things you're saying goodbye to for leading you to this version of yourself.

WANING CRESCENT *transition, healing,*

The thing about containing so many multitudes of moods and feelings is that you know all about emerging from one state into another. This ability to shake things off—to cycle through soft and hard, transparent and opaque—is a chameleon gift. Think of the reassuring constancy of the tides rolling in and out at sea. Each time they come in, they bear new gifts of pearly shells, strange and tangled seaweeds, messages in ancient bottles. What work have you put in and sent out to the world? What rewards and payoffs are ready to be called in? Make a collage of your moods during this time, tracking them like the tides, noting the songs and colors and poems that illuminate them. What do you notice about the way they ebb and flow?

Mood Phase Horoscopes

ROMANCE

There's a part of you that needs the reassurance of being loved like fish need water. The rub is that it can take forever to trust someone enough to let them see the whole you, and in the meantime, you probe with your thousands of invisible jelly tentacles to test and make sure you won't be left with your tender parts exposed. Consider the fact that humans are ever changing, and this means we are fallible, flawed, and fickle. Try to notice the inscrutable words, actions, and support that people do show to tell you they love you. Practice breathing through the scary sensations of falling, of clenching and unclenching your fists and muscles, until you can feel like a soft sponge, ready to absorb the love that was meant for you.

CHANGE

Who are you when you're wholly attuned to the fluctuating moods and feelings that sweep in and out of you? When you can observe yourself from this distance, you can allow yourself to notice how there are so many shades, versions, colors, musical notes, clouds, and sunsets inside of you. It can be hard to find your balance when wading through the deep end of them. When you see yourself slipping down into the quicksand of your emotions, practice thinking of yourself as a kaleidoscope. Write out this reflection: "There's a part of me that feels _____." By recognizing that it is not the whole of you, you can gain some perspective; you can see how this part is linked into the entire multifaceted notion of you. Try to greet each dimension of yourself with curiosity and kindness.

COMPASSION

To be as absorbent as this part of you is means that you are open to soaking up the spectrum of humanity and its emotions. The risk is that true compassion requires some emotional distance in order to not take on someone else's pain entirely as your own—because then the entire ship can sink. Your spongy qualities mean that you are the definition of a true listener, constantly searching for ways you can relate and connect. This vulnerable availability can make others feel safe and at home in your presence, truly seen and accepted for all their flaws and teetering doubts. Remember that allowing others to see the strange, dark depths of your feelings allows compassion to run both ways. What parts of you need tenderness and understanding right now?

REFLECTION

Have you ever just blissfully floated in a body of water? Mysterious undercurrents move, and the creatures that live in them learn to move with them rather than exhaust themselves. There's a part of you that has the same gift—seeing where the motions of your feelings take you and sitting with them. This ability gives you a knack for inhabiting these spaces completely, like an octopus changing color to match the surrounding rocks. Your dreams can offer you a different kind of map, in which you can investigate the subconscious currents that drive your waking hours. Take note when you wake up of the different moods, emotions, tenors of your dreams. Give them each a different color and rather than write them down, paint them.

● ● SUFFERING ● ● ●

The problem with getting stuck in your feelings when the tides sweep in is that you can get shipwrecked by them. Remember that elation and depression are simply two different currents, pulling you on different trajectories. The trick is to not get lost in the murk but, rather, to recognize that as swiftly as currents arrive, so they can leave. We live in a society that puts currency in presenting a happy front. This can put you at odds with the world and your place in it, and this is okay—let yourself bob along at your own emotional pace. When you align yourself with the innate and mercurial rhythms of your moods, you can become better able to recognize them as the fleeting, constantly flowing things they are.

 ## STAGNATION

Think of a ship lost at sea, bobbing fitfully at the mercy of the waves. When you feel this enveloping lostness, this overwhelming feeling of being a speck in such a wild and unforgiving world, give yourself the outlet of creating something to guide you through it. Paint your way out of it, write your way out of it, surf your way out of it, sing your way out of it. Remember that you can also be a lighthouse, if only you can find the internal light to flash you in a different direction. Keep a running list of the things, people, places, songs, and colors that can serve as anchors, that keep you feeling moored and safe even when you can't tell which direction is which.

 ## ACTION

When your currency is your emotions, it can be hard to let go of things you have feelings about, even if those things happened long ago. People and memories are sticky, they leave a residue that can linger, and it can be easy and familiar to get stuck in these old moods. Try paying attention to the fluctuations of your environment. Are you feeling lonely? Overwhelmed? Worn out? If you're feeling stuck in your thoughts, try moving your body by stretching or walking or striking weird, unfamiliar poses. Ask the people closest to you to help you notice when you're just treading water, looking exhausted, or waiting for a current to move you along. Sometimes you just need a gentle push.

 ## FEAR

Fear is a strange emotion: It presents as a reaction in your body. Fear is also linked to loss—we're often afraid of what we stand to lose, of the risks of our emotional investments, of losing a part of ourselves in another person. Fear is the recognition that our feelings are involved, and that makes us vulnerable. When you feel fear in your body, try to stop and note what it is that you feel you are losing. Is it control? Another person? A way of life that is transitioning? Rather than retreat to where nothing can touch you, allow fear to crack you open, to make you a little bit curious about why you are clinging so tightly to something that you might need to let go of.

Altar

This season, use your altar to reflect on your relationship with safety of all kinds—personal, collective, and intimate.

Decorate your altar with silvery whites and blues, invoking the moon.

Call upon crustaceans, shelled creatures, and saltwater and freshwater beasts.

Place offerings of seashells, bowls of water, teapots, umbrellas, photos of loved ones, homes past and present, images pertaining to your ancestry.

Complete your altar by building yourself a cozy nest for you to retreat to this season.

Affirmations

I nurture and provide for the ones I love.

I protect and hold close all that is sacred to me.

I take responsibility for the depths and gnarled roots of my heritage.

I trust in my chosen definitions of home and family.

Rituals

PEN PALS

Write a letter to a person who has hurt or betrayed you. Say all the things you want to say. Do not send this letter. Write a second letter from the perspective of your betrayer, assuming they received your first letter. Say the things you want to hear. Write a third letter from a speculative third party who has been watching you both. Say the things you need to hear. Burn all three letters. Forgive yourself; you may choose whether to forgive anyone else. Write your letter of forgiveness here.

SYNCHRONICITIES

This month, be a sponge for all the universe has to say. Note whenever themes, images, words, signs, and symbols repeat. Which ones are guiding you along? Which ones make you stop in your tracks? Which ones are natural, which ones are a stretch to anyone but you? Synchronicity is a two-way conversation with the universe. Map out your landscape of synchronicities and see what you can intuit from the shape it forms. Draw it here.

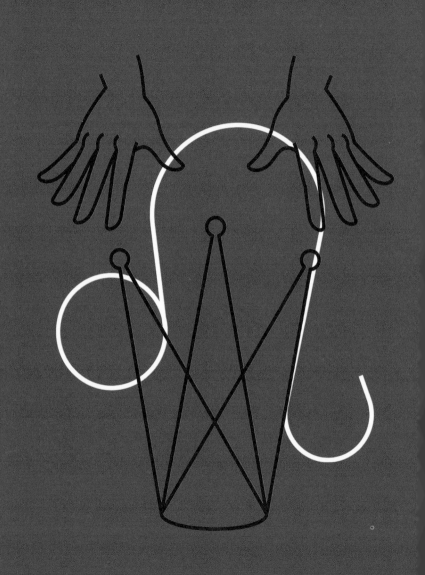

Leo

JULY 24—AUGUST 23
Fifth House of Expression

Is there a more self-possessed creature on the planet than a cat? Like a cat, this part of you knows exactly how much space you want to take up when you walk in a room, and it's usually a lot. It can't be helped; it can feel as if you're a glowing magnet emitting sparks. The more eyes on you the better. What's more, it can make you the epitome of reinvention, inhabiting each incarnation of yourself fully and expansively. People can't help but be drawn to that kind of authenticity, and they can envy the way you easily inhabit your skin. The one thing that can be hard to see, sometimes, is how a blind belief in yourself can get in between you and others, particularly if you feel threatened or dismissed. It can be hard to listen to criticism, but sometimes it's what's required of you in order to make it to the next level of being. The upside is that you are always the first one to jump through the fire if that is what's necessary. In this way you dare everyone around you to be their bravest selves too. Remember that you will always thrive when you're grounded in your own sense of self.

CONSTELLATION
The Lion

ELEMENT
Fire

RULING PLANET
Sun

QUALITY
Fixed

Moon Phase Horoscopes

NEW MOON *rest, recuperation, beginnings*

Taking a moment to pause can be hard, especially when you've got places to go and people to be. Who are you when no one is paying attention? You're still you. In fact, you can learn a lot by listening, by noticing, just for a minute. Try to slow down a little. Live in the still, awkward pauses in conversations, the moments when no one is looking at you. In order to regenerate to your fullest powers and to be a better friend to yourself and to others, give yourself some time to empty out, if only to try on the foreign feeling that comes with it. Give yourself a mind-set of curiosity to figure out where your itchiness comes from, when it finally does. Can you give the roots of that itchiness a name, a face, a reason?

WAXING CRESCENT *energy, initiative, activation*

This is a time when something big and slow is finding its way to you. It may not show up all at once; it might seep into your life in ways that are hard to notice. Pay attention to the way this sensation kick-starts your heart, the way it makes the hairs on your arm stand up. Clear your conscience for this newness by telling people how you really feel. Let the heat inside you melt every icy sorrow, let it forge a space that can fit your whole messy self. If anyone knows the key to merging all your parts into a total reinvention it's you, but it can't be rushed or messily glued together. Practice by finding something methodical to build—something that requires sorting, categorizing, painstaking attention. Then apply it to yourself.

FIRST QUARTER *balance, focus, commitment*

WAXING GIBBOUS *patience, cultivation, fine-tuning*

Sometimes it can be easier to feel that you're lacking something than to accept that it's a constant challenge to live up to the fullest version of yourself. Sometimes it's easier to not hold out hope than to accept the desire that can ache in your bones. Our wants and desires can shift; our definitions of who we want to be can change at any time. This is a time to call upon your famous courage. Watch videos of wild animals in nature and notice how they have zero self-doubt in their graceful movements. Practice holding these poses and attitudes yourself. When you feel uncertain or as if you don't know how to take up new space, be an animal. Make weird faces in the mirror and see who emerges.

Slowing down can be difficult when you have so much energy to burn. Why worry about the details when you can keep moving, shifting, and taking shape? Cultivating patience with yourself, others, and projects is understanding that sometimes things just need to take the time they're going to take. You can't force a bud to bloom or a cloudless sky to rain. Allowing for things to unfold on their own timeline can teach you something about your own unfolding. What is currently happening that requires your patience? Practice sitting still every morning for five minutes, letting your mind think all its thoughts. Take a few deep breaths and notice how your thoughts support you in slowing down, just for a minute.

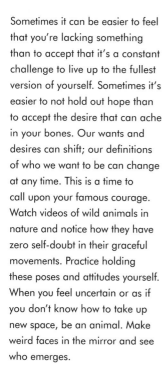

FULL MOON *completion, fulfillment, abundance*

WANING GIBBOUS *review, reflection, introspection*

You haven an uncanny knack for dreaming big and then living those dreams into reality. What are your deepest, most secret desires at this time? How might you be getting in your own way or making the path ahead murkier than it needs to be? When you settle deeply into yourself and separate from your need to be noticed, what truths emerge? If you're looking for abundance, practice giving it away to others first. See how it feels to give and not take. Giving what it is that you desire is its own spell; it creates an energy that magnetizes you to the generosities that are meant for you. Sending your magnetism out to others for good can only double back to you, eventually, when you least expect it.

It's not always easy to look back and then to let it go. Sometimes it's the drama itself that feeds the ego, all sharp teeth and crumbs, a hungry ghost that will never feel full. But something profound can happen when you learn from the heartaches of the past: They can act as tiny flares that will guide your way forward, nudging you a bit more quickly past those same old obstacles. The hungry ghost will learn to stop searching for crumbs of validation, and you'll learn to let go so that you can fill yourself up with the here and now, with the bright shimmering future. Right now is a time to satisfy yourself with the things, places, and people that push you forward, that make you expand to meet the future versions of you.

LAST QUARTER *discarding, amends, adjustment*

WANING CRESCENT *transition, healing, closure*

Sometimes exits are just as important as entrances. How can you do justice to the things that have brought you this far? Think of a nesting doll—there are many versions of you that came before, that brought you to this very place and time. They played the starring role in the movie of your life and then left the stage for the next version to appear. Sometimes the past doesn't want to let us go, however; it waits in the wings, watching for a place to enter and shout, "I told you so!" when you make the same mistakes, date the wrong people, and so on. So write an exit scene for the old versions of you that get in the way. Thank them for the ways they try to protect you. Then write them off your show.

The life you've been living is going to shake like a snow globe. And no one is more prepared than you to embrace the unknown and to let the flakes fall where they may. What can you loosen your grip on and allow to unfold the way it wants to? Sometimes looking away allows something to bloom unexpectedly, to make the final twist in its unfolding. Think about all the things that feel just out of reach that you've been yearning for. What would it feel like to unfurl toward them, slowly and deliberately? How can you get out of your own way? Try to imagine the infinite outcomes of your decisions; imagine the things that lie on the other side of the question mark. Remember that they are all possible.

Mood Phase Horoscopes

ROMANCE

We all worry that we are at once both easy and impossible to love.
There is a part of you that demands recognition of how easy it is to
love you, yet a part of you also knows that your ego can search for a
limitless supply of validation. Knowing your own worth without the spot-
light of others on you is the best place to stand when deciding who is
allowed to move into your heart. When you let yourself become parched
because you're feeling needy, try tapping into the quiet things you can
do to make yourself feel loved. Rather than search for affection, notice
the other ways you can fill yourself. When you meet others in that space,
you're more likely to encounter something real and true.

FEAR

There is a part of you whose biggest fear comes from feeling unseen,
unworthy, and invisible. Often the root of this fear lies in a fixed notion
of what it means to be the opposite of those things and defining yourself
against that notion. How can you become more fluid in your ideas
about what these things feel like and look like? What do your fears have
to teach you about your strengths? You are constantly changing; to keep
up with yourself, you'll have to adapt to the shifting meanings of what it
means to be seen and worthy. It requires being able to adjust your sails
and move in a different, better, clearer direction so that you can gain
some perspective and clarity.

REFLECTION

In order to fully inhabit your most authentic self, you'll need to understand how you've gotten to be this you, in this moment. Among the gifts of this part of you is your undiluted sense of self and the ease with which you inhabit it. At times it can almost feel as though you are playing yourself in a movie, with your lines already written. When you experience these moments of déjà vu, stop to ask yourself where this repetition stems from, and if it still feels authentic. How have you grown, shrunk, or cast things off? Practice taking a picture of yourself every day for a month and reflect on the small changes you see. What story do these photos have to tell you about your own growth?

CONNECTION

Who are you without an audience? There's a part of you that truly comes alive in the presence of others. It highlights your innate theatricality: the easy way you can take up space and turn up the volume and brightness in every room you enter. This isn't to say your friendships are a one-way street of admiration; rather, once someone has proven their worth, you can return the favor with loyalty and generosity. In fact, it's through friendships that the egoless side of yourself can truly come to life because you feel seen. Remember to give back the admiration and attention you crave. It's in those moments of true give-and-take that your genuine sincerity can shine, drawing others into your enveloping warmth and authenticity.

ANGER

There's a part of you that is constantly setting the bar higher and higher for yourself—it's the kind of evolution and reinvention you thrive on. If you're not careful, though, you may find yourself feeling chronically dissatisfied with the present moment, a kind of locational itchiness that keeps you from fully living in this current version of yourself. Remember that a part of yourself has the ability to understand that you only get braver by knowing the role of the past in your current situation. The next time you feel angry, see if you can locate the source and where in time and space it exists. If it's not in the present, there's not much you can do about it other than practice living until you arrive in that moment.

ACTION

There's a side of you that hates being still, is allergic to inertia and lethargy, and wants to always keep moving forward, into the brightest light possible that can refract your growth back to you. The catch is that your drive comes from your own volition, and not from the urging of others. When you feel yourself growing resentful out of a sense of obligation, see if you can remind yourself of the mutual exchange that is present in any kind of partnership—romantic, creative, or professional. How can you allow for the sense of expansion that comes from investing in others alongside yourself and from holding yourself accountable to them? It's largely through compromise with others that we are able to grow into our full strengths.

 ## WORK

What does it mean to be a true and inspiring collaborator? Though there's a part of you that would prefer to be the main character in all the dramas of your life, it takes a certain grace to allow others to occupy the stage and to co-create. When you view your worth through the lens of scarcity or competition, you risk walling yourself off to the light that can bounce off others and back onto you. Remember that the more you can selflessly contribute to the greater good of whatever you are working toward, the fuller you will feel and the more connected you will become to it. Your strength lies in the fact that you bring a uniqueness that is not copied from another template—you are the origin.

STRENGTH

Many people are drawn to this part of you precisely because of the forceful, effortless strength that you radiate. When you are centered wholly in yourself, you can radiate a palpable confidence and allure that commands others to sit up and pay attention. Like all powers, it can be used for both good and evil: manipulation and ego boosting or inspiration and motivation. How can you tell the difference between the two? When you lend your strength to others in order to boost them higher as well, you'll feel an electric, brimming excitement in your bones. Memorize that feeling. Anything less, and it's worth examining your motives. Remember to share these rare gifts. When you are generous with your strength, it will be returned to you fivefold through admiration and inspiration.

Altar

This season, use your altar as a stage for all that makes you shine and glow.

Decorate your altar with golds and oranges, invoking the sun.

Call upon regal, glamorous beasts and felines of all sizes.

Place offerings of confetti and sequins, things that sparkle and glint, costume parts, art supplies, artifacts and images from your childhood.

Charge your altar by blessing it with an improvisational performance for you and you alone.

Affirmations

I open myself to expressing my inner light.

I accept my role as the courageous ruler of my life story.

I honor my inner child and give them what they need to thrive.

I am my most beloved when I am generous and humble.

Rituals

TALISMAN ARCHIVE

Photograph belongings that have a mysterious sentiment for you; choose nothing too overt. For each one, write a description of its powers and the elements/emotions it governs. The next time you need help, consult your photographs and reread the descriptions you wrote below. Choose the talisman required and carry it with you in secret. Don't worry; it knows what to do.

_____

_____

_____

_____

_____

_____

_____

_____

_____

_____

INNER-CHILD COSPLAY

Think back to your most formative childhood self, the one who held all the power and wisdom and innocence before you were hardened or diluted by the ways of the world and growing older or by boxes and boundaries drawn by others around you. What did you want to be when you grew up? What were the lofty aspirations you had before they were taken down a notch by practicality and adulthood? Write down descriptions of those pure aspirational selves. Create from those descriptions a list of things you still do and still own that reflect the essence of these selves, and from that list, create a costume, wardrobe, or armor. For the next month, you will cosplay as this childhood dream, however theatrical or subtle as fits with your life. Draw those pure aspirational selves here.

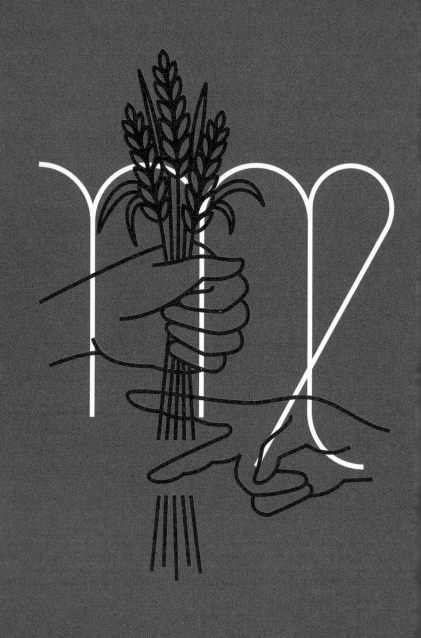

Virgo

Sometimes it's exhausting to be locked into such a tit-for-tat war between your feelings and your thoughts. If only everyone knew how tender you are beneath all that practicality! Sometimes your acute sensitivity is mistaken for sharp observational skills only, when the fact is that one is endlessly informing the other. You're the first person your friends go to when they need advice and an obsessive eye for detail. But sometimes that famous perfectionism can be your worst enemy when you turn it on yourself, leading you to become your worst critic. The problem, sometimes, is both you and the world around you are constantly shifting, demanding fluid rules and boundaries. Although you don't like leaving anything to chance, life is often exactly that—chance. It's when you turn your practicality outward that you benefit greatly, for you take great pleasure in being helpful and taking care of people and things. You just want to know how all the puzzle pieces fit before you dump them out of the box—you want a plan, and this can make you a little bit apprehensive before committing to people and things.

CONSTELLATION
The Maiden

ELEMENT
Earth

RULING PLANET
Mercury

QUALITY
Mutable

Moon Phase Horoscopes

NEW MOON *rest, recuperation, beginnings*

WAXING CRESCENT *energy, initiative, activation*

This is a time to let the busy channels in your brain go dark for a moment to recalibrate. There's a part of your mind that can be a constant buzz of worry, vigilance, and to-do lists. But if you take the space to allow yourself a moment of rest, notice the strange sense that deep down, you'll probably be just fine if you let down your guard and know that you have your own back. To practice this strange commitment to nothingness, find an old to-do list that you've already completed. Look at it and remember the pleasure of being able to rest at the top of the mountain of finished tasks before beginning all over again the next day. See if you can stretch this feeling for five more minutes.

There's a part of you that lives to put in the work of laying solid foundations in order to build something true and real. This means that sometimes you have to keep searching for the answers that feel as if they're hovering just out of reach. The problem is that the harder you look, the fuzzier they appear. Often this is because you think you've solved this problem before, but it may be wisest to be the fool and forget what you think you know. Think about how sometimes the answers appear before you even know what the questions are. Imagine someone gave you a hammer you didn't ask for. What would you nail to the wall? You have all the tools you need, even if their purpose isn't clear to you yet.

FIRST QUARTER *balance, focus, commitment*

WAXING GIBBOUS *patience, cultivation, fine-tuning*

It can be so easy to talk yourself out of taking necessary risks in order to grow. Risk often means a loss of control. Often this part of you tries to move straight through the spaces that scare you as quickly as possible. But sometimes those spaces have things to teach you, secret tests, and hidden trophies. Try making a list of the things that give you strength and courage. Sometimes those things might be your dog, or a tattered old underlined book, or the way the sky looks at 5 A.M. Remember that no matter how prepared you think you are, things will always find a way to surprise you with their variables. Lean into the surprises, make room for them, let them expand you and your future bigger than you ever thought possible.

This is a time for slowing down, for looking at the granular aspect of things. Examine the textures of your life with a magnifying glass. This is where the details you live for can take on a vibrant, buzzing life of their own, where you can watch them expand into their purpose like a sponge taking shape in water. Even though you'd rather move with brisk efficiency, experiment with what it feels like to slow down and allow things to atomize on their own timeline. Try going outside and finding a handful of oddly shaped rocks. Take the time to think of how you can categorize them by shape, size, texture, and mood. Try out a few different sorting methods. How can you sort the other details of your life in a similar way to see what patterns emerge?

FULL MOON *completion, fulfillment, abundance*

What sense of fullness can you tap into in order to feel connected to the things you are creating? Whether it's work, love, friendship, or creativity, connect to the root of the well that sparks reassurance in your own decisions. Remember that intuition is just another layer of data that can help you record impressions and gut reactions. It's there to be trusted just as much as any number or statistic, but it's a muscle that needs to be used as much as any other to stay sharp and strong. When confronted by any choice that makes your heart beat fast, ask: Does my decision make me feel warmer or colder? Let that simple internal thermometer take the temperature of your desires. Move toward what feels right.

WANING GIBBOUS *review, reflection, introspection*

Think about how many things you cram into your life, the way your feelings shift, and the space they occupy in your body. Think about what you need to get rid of and what you need to make space for. Sometimes life develops tiny frictions, like a bad tooth we try to chew around. Months can pass before we realize how we've slowly accommodated a silent, blooming pain. Now is a good time to reflect on this collection of grievances you've accumulated yet haven't dealt with. Imagine them jumping off a cliff like tiny snarling gremlins. Then try to relax into everything that's coming your way; welcome it into all this new space you've freed up. Use your tingly senses to find new ways to think, to be, to feel.

LAST QUARTER *discarding, amends, adjustment*

WANING CRESCENT *transition, healing, closure*

Be prepared to shatter some boarded-up walls in yourself. There might be some ghosts lurking behind there, all hungry and alone. Often we lock them away, unsure of how to begin—yet we are always aware of their presence. Before you let these ghosts go, ask them what they need in order to be released. What can you say to them to give them the goodbye they deserve? Sometimes ghosts want you to remember what you've tried to forget, sometimes they just have a final message for you. Sometimes you have to clean up the mess they made. Just remember to be patient and kind with the lonely things you find behind those walls. Turn their parting words into art, into songs, into stories.

There are so many quietly industrious animals: mice, bees, and beavers. They are creatures that appreciate the diligence of daily work that adds up to something larger than its parts, like a beehive or dam. They focus on things that make a home, or a job, or a relationship. Rarely do they pause to reflect on how their hard work has paid off—there's just always something else to attend to. Yet sometimes taking a beat before moving on to the next thing in order to measure how far you've come can serve you far more than working to stay busy. Think back to the beginning of this cycle: Who were you then? Who are you now? What will you take with you, and how can you thank yourself when no one else will?

Mood Phase Horoscopes

 **ROMANCE**

Most people like to think of love as an all-encompassing affair of the heart. Most people, conversely, struggle with the day-to-day, minute-to-minute atomization of love. There are numerous small acts of devotion. This is where this part of you shines; it loves to be of service to express the mountain of your feelings in sizeable tasks. Some might mistake this for something less grand, but what they don't realize is that life is the small moments that add up to something larger than the sum of its parts. This part of you is ever-vigilant in guarding your love and keeping it safe. Love for you is a duty to be cherished, to be taken seriously, and to be a steady, beating thing just like your heart. Practice the art of using words, as well as actions, to demonstrate the feelings that bubble below the surface.

 **REFLECTION**

There's a part of you that relishes breaking down information into its many data points to see its microscopic parts. You have a finely-tuned understanding of the way things work both internally and externally. It also means this part of you can have a hard time zooming out, taking the bird's-eye view, or seeing your whole self in all its contradictory, complex glory. How can you extend some kindness to these parts of you, to help them understand how deeply connected they are to the rest? See if your reflections can take on the tone of acceptance and self-compassion rather than criticism. How can you get out of your own way so that all these parts of you can breathe and grow?

ACTION

How do the things you do inform the person you are? This is a part of you that thrives on learning information with which you can take action, rather than deal in abstractions and feelings. Time is something everyone approaches differently, and one approach is to maximize each minute through systems and structures and routines. This is an incredibly valuable skill, but take care not to become so rigid that you can't accept others' approach to time. The next time you feel yourself going taut like a snapped rubber band, try relaxing your body inch by inch and counting to sixty. When you're done, notice how the world is still moving, breathing, grinding along underneath you. It won't stop just because you did.

 ## STAGNATION

Imagine a tractor stuck in the mud. The more it grinds its wheels, the more entrenched it becomes. There's a part of you that has this tendency to panic the moment you sense you've become stuck too. But the truth is that sometimes the challenge is to walk away for a bit in order to come back to the problem with new eyes. This might cause you moments of sweaty angst. When you find yourself in this place, write a list of all the times you've been stuck or unsure how to proceed—in work, in love, in creativity. Look at each thing. Did you eventually get unstuck? Did you find a different path to certainty? Or did you walk away because it wasn't worth your energy?

CONNECTION

There are certainly qualities in friendships that guarantee longevity. One of those qualities is consistency—the kind of quiet showing up that allows people to feel those invisible seams of what it really means to be supported. This is a part of you that knows the currency of patience. People often forget how much they take for granted in their friendships until they run into trouble or heartache. Yet your outward sense of detachment allows you to see the longer arc of things and to realize that it's the small actions that water the soil that makes friendships grow and endure. This part of you knows that sometimes, it merely takes just showing up and sitting with someone in their uncertainty.

 ## STRENGTH

Have you ever watched ants on a sidewalk, all lined up with their marching orders and mysterious ant tasks? Ants know that it takes a village to get things done, with each ant playing its part. There's a part of you that knows something about this too—about checking items off a list, making sure each detail is perfect. Even if no one else sees it, you know it's there, and it's a rare satisfaction to be able to derive such joy in the unseen. Living by one's feelings has its benefits, but life often requires an analytical mind to get through the days. See if you can allow yourself the benefit of recognizing these talents you have to offer the world around you.

FEAR

If there's one universal emotion besides love, it's fear, even if we try to board up the doors against it. But fear is nearly always a by-product of something else, and it's worth inviting it inside in its scary costume and asking why it has suddenly shown up. Try to take fear's costume off. What worry is underneath? What can be hard for this part of you is that fear is an emotion that doesn't often respond to rationality. Often the only way to talk to your fears is in the language of feelings—not of rational thinking. The next time you're afraid, write a list. On one side, write: "I think _____." On the other, write "I feel _____." Keep writing until your feelings and your thoughts find some common ground.

WORK

There's a part of you that finds a strong identity in the work you do. In many ways, this ethic is where you get your worth. The contradiction lies in the fact that often you can hold yourself (and others) to nearly impossible standards of detailed perfection, and it can become easy to get bogged down in the minutiae rather than see the bigger picture. If you hold too tightly to the details, you miss opportunities that arise that can move you in different, better directions. The next time the direction changes, rather than go rigid, allow yourself to imagine the other outcomes, even if doing so means relinquishing some control. Your talent is in the ability to find a productive rhythm quickly and to figure out the quickest solutions effortlessly.

Altar

This season, use your altar to pay tribute to your purpose and craft.

Decorate your altar with minimal and natural earth tones,
invoking the utilitarian and hand hewn.

Call upon meticulous creatures with specialized skills and routines.

Place offerings of whole grains, nuts and seeds, tools and equipment,
pottery and ceramics, handcrafted items, organizers and to-do lists.

Visit your altar with regular sets of gentle stretches and
whispers of gratitude to your physicality.

Affirmations

I choose when to be in control and when to let go.

I honor my mind, body, and spirit with what nourishes me most.

I hone in on my natural gifts and strive to improve them.

I release the need for perfection and focus on maximizing good.

Rituals

MAGIC WORD

Take a piece of paper and write the entire alphabet on it three times, leaving space between the letters. Cut the sheet into small squares of one letter each. Try to savor this meditative exercise, to really take your time instead of rushing through. When you are done, place your letters in a vessel. Without looking, draw out thirteen letters. Arrange them into a word or words, real or made up. Say the word or words out loud, feeling them roll off your tongue. Repeat them until you can remember them without friction. Write them down here. Call upon these magic words when you need a breakthrough.

THE SHAPE OF WORRY

Take a pen and close your eyes for a moment. Hold a worry in your mind, something you've been turning over and over with no resolution. Can you feel it in your skin, all buzzing and alive? Take your pen and, beginning anywhere on the page, start to draw a shape. Any shape will do. Keep adding to the shape: strange geometries, lines that go nowhere. Keep drawing until you feel the worry dissipate, or until the answer to your worry begins to take shape. Sometimes the answer is just to find some momentary peace.

Libra

Seventh House of Relation

The world needs more peacemakers, diplomats, and balancers. These people can see every nuanced side of an argument and find the tiny, crystallized points where they meet and can be settled. It doesn't hurt that nearly everyone likes a person who can be so malleable, and who makes it their business to be likeable. Yet this graciousness can get this part of you into trouble, both with others and with yourself. When you attune yourself to others—whether to keep the peace or get attention—you risk losing a small but essential part of yourself. This can make you fundamentally unknowable: You tend to become a bit of a shapeshifter depending on the company. Part of this motivation to please is a profound dislike of being alone, but you also have an idealized version of whom you'd like to be. Your challenge is to find your authentic, true self and operate from that grounded space. Often we tend to want to see an emotion reflected back to us in order to feel that it's valid. But the truth is that you can just spend some time looking in the mirror at your own reflection—and talk to who you see in it.

CONSTELLATION
The Scales

ELEMENT
Air

RULING PLANET
Venus

QUALITY
Cardinal

Moon Phase Horoscopes

NEW MOON *rest, recuperation, beginnings*

Minutes might stretch too long to see a future or run too short to catch your breath. Try not to let this knock you off kilter. Time shifts according to how new or old an experience feels. You don't need to figure out every piece of every puzzle of your life, and you don't have to know what's going to happen next. Let yourself be still while you watch it unfold in its own sweet time. Try not to judge what you see, and try not to control how fast or slow it happens. Being alone with uncertainty can be hard—it's so much easier to distract yourself, to keep in constant motion like a flitting hummingbird. But sometimes the only thing that can really fill you up is your own ability to become the blank page.

WAXING CRESCENT *energy, initiative, activation*

Look around your life for the holes, for the empty spaces, for the things that are missing. Even if you're feeling complacent, even if you don't want to face them, these wants might shake you up, catch you off guard, and change the rules of your existence. Try not to be afraid of them, even if they open you up. Instead, think of them as an invitation to your own curiosity. When you approach something out of curiosity rather than need or yearning, it allows you the space to examine it through the intersection of your heart and your mind. Can you locate the source of emptiness it might fill up? How does the idea of doing something new make you feel? Where might you begin to do the work it requires?

FIRST QUARTER *balance, focus, commitment*

WAXING GIBBOUS *patience, cultivation, fine-tuning*

What if you just pretended you were brave until it felt true? Try walking down your street as if nothing could ever scare you, even if it does, especially if it does. Begin to believe in the things that shimmer around the edges of your dreams. Usually those are the things trying to poke through the defenses your mind puts up against perceived threats. If you try this, you might feel vulnerable in your newfound attempts at bravery and that can leave you feeling shaky. Don't try to snuff out the tenderness inside you; don't try to build a moat around your wobbliness. Let those things be your map—the things that make you feel most soft are actually the things pointing you in the right direction.

Maintaining your sense of balance also means you have the grace to know when to hoist your sails in order to go with the direction of the wind, rather than flail against it. If you look at a ship, it's constructed in such a way as to weather the harshest of storms. What similar fortifications can you build to allow yourself to stay upright even when you get knocked around? Sometimes this might require you to work on creating your own inner compass rather than choose a side to appease someone. Practice rehearsing this feeling by standing somewhere windy and feeling your own center of gravity. Notice how there is always a still, steady center of yourself that you can return to over and over.

FULL MOON *completion, fulfillment, abundance*

WANING GIBBOUS *review, reflection, introspection*

There's a part of you that wants to believe that the world comes down to good or evil, black or white, all or nothing. That once the scales are tipped, one side will bow under its weight. But what if the world can also be seen as an overlay of colors, a plaid that mixes sweetness and pain? Sometimes it's worth admitting that things are more complicated and murky than they seem. Now is a time to dig deep into your intuition in order to make space for a possible third path that's neither one side nor the other. Try this strange feeling out by taking two colors of paint and mixing them together to see the gradation of feelings and truths that can happen in this world.

Your brain and your heart are constantly battling it out, competing for attention, presenting contradicting evidence for all kinds of scenarios. But what if you could remind them that they are working toward the same ultimate end? There can be a balance between facts and feelings; there can be a space in which both stories are true. This is a time to pause and hear both sides of the issues they're doing battle over. Make a two-column chart across a full page. Let your brain tell you what to write about it on one side, and let your heart guide you on the other. Keep writing until they can find a resolution. Remind yourself that what they have in common is your own best interest.

LAST QUARTER *discarding, amends, adjustment*

WANING CRESCENT *transition, healing, closure*

Is there something you're secretly hoping someone else will give you that you don't think you can give yourself? So often we wait for permission without even knowing that's what we're doing. Imagine for a moment that you may in fact be the gatekeeper of your desires. In order to allow this attitude to unfurl, you'll need to make amends with the parts of yourself that don't trust your own capabilities, your own abandonment to your needs. Write a list of all the secret yearnings in your heart; write until you're blue in face and out of breath. Then write a letter to yourself about all the reasons why you deserve those things, and the ways you can give them to yourself.

Sometimes when we act in accordance with what we are trying to bring into the world, the resources we need to accomplish it mysteriously show up. What can you call out for in the quiet void that can help you expand your sense of self? It's true that sometimes a part of you likes to stay in a liminal space for as long as possible, afraid to disappoint anyone and looking everywhere but your own sweet brain for directions. But you might find that if you move confidently toward the path that makes you feel warm and expansive, the objects you need to feel confident will begin to appear in strange and unlikely places, as if they were just waiting for you to show up.

Mood Phase Horoscopes

ROMANCE

There's a part of you that was built for searching for another who can balance you. There's nothing wrong with seeking the sense of wholeness that can come from a true partnership. There is a risk, though, in seeking love for its own sake. Being alone can be hard. But love is also terrifying in its insistence on blind trust. Check in with yourself to make sure your longing for romance isn't merely a need to be distracted. It's wonderful to have ideals, but remember that everyone is also figuring it out as they go. Even though it can be scary, practice the art of being alone and complete in the skin you're in. Take yourself out on dates, all alone. Then notice the different energies you attract.

 ### CONNECTION

There is a real strength and benefit in being the person others turn to when things need to be settled peacefully. In this way, this part of you is indispensable. But if you bend too far in the direction of pleasing people, you begin to lose some of the admiration you've earned. Your attunement to others is a real strength, as is your natural instinct for bringing people together. Practice rehearsing your true feelings and opinions with yourself, even if they make your heart race and your throat dry. Tell your feelings to one friend and notice how your confiding opened an invisible portal that made something between you both more spacious and solid. Keep practicing this with the other people in your life until it becomes natural.

REFLECTION

Did you know that the mirror is one of the talismans of Libras? The trick is in learning how to accept what you notice staring back at you. The benefit of truly being able to see yourself is that it allows you to step into the next version of yourself. This part of you can have a tendency to want to see yourself through the eyes of others, to seek worth there. For now, though, practice reflecting from a place that feels like the center of your own gravity and blur out everyone in the background. Stare into your mirror, and when you notice yourself judging, say those words out loud so you can hear them with your own voice: *Thinking. Judging.* This habit can steer you toward true reflection.

ANGER

Anger isn't always about what it seems, which is why so many people struggle to confront or control it. There's a part of you that feels your blood race, all panicky, when you sense anger in yourself or someone else. Anger can be a destabilizer, but it can also be a release, a gateway to whatever emotion lies underneath and is driving it. Remember: In these moments, anger is rarely an enduring emotion—it burns itself out quickly. Don't be so quick to appease others or diffuse conflict if the anger is necessary to get to the bottom of things. When you feel anger, locate the source and the other emotions connected to it. Check in with your own feelings first before asking others to validate it.

● ⚬ SUFFERING ● ⚬ ⚬

How do birds know how to return to their homes each night? When you are attuned to your own place within the world, it becomes easier to find your sense of direction. It's when you look to other people to point the way that this part of you can become turned around. If you are finding it hard to notice where your feet touch the ground, do the things that return you to yourself. Surround yourself with the people who know you best, even the uncertain parts of you. They will be honored that you trust them enough to not be okay around them. The next time you feel lost, check to make sure you're not arranging your face into a mask that covers up your pain.

 ## STAGNATION

Have you ever seen a balancing scale? You could go on forever adding things to each side in order to make them perfectly even. Yet life is rarely ever so cut and dry. There's a part of you that can become paralyzed by inertia with the worry that you'll make the wrong choice. Try not to make yourself so malleable that you're forever trying to calibrate this messy thing called life. Practice the art of making a decision without asking for someone else's advice first. Making decisions is like using a muscle— the more you use it, the more reflexive it becomes. Don't make tedious lists of pros and cons but do practice the art of using your intuition first, and examining the outcome later.

COMPASSION

It takes a true sense of fairness and justice to embody real compassion. This is a part of you that is highly sensitive to injustice and can't stand for inequality. What offers you a rare grace is a cool-headed intellect that allows you to be a genuine guardian of peace and balance. This part of you has the ability to inhabit compassion through your intellect rather than through your emotions, and it gives you the rare gift of being able to cut through an argument with detached logic, facts, and deliberations. To be able to locate the center of all sides is a gift. Remember to extend this worldly compassion to yourself as well, to see how you are also deserving of having your own solid voice and views.

STRENGTH

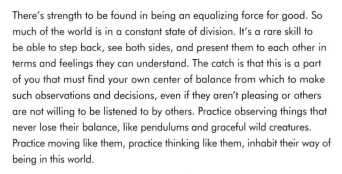

There's strength to be found in being an equalizing force for good. So much of the world is in a constant state of division. It's a rare skill to be able to step back, see both sides, and present them to each other in terms and feelings they can understand. The catch is that this is a part of you that must find your own center of balance from which to make such observations and decisions, even if they aren't pleasing or others are not willing to be listened to by others. Practice observing things that never lose their balance, like pendulums and graceful wild creatures. Practice moving like them, practice thinking like them, inhabit their way of being in this world.

Altar

This season, use your altar as a sanctuary for your inner quiet.

Decorate your altar with pale rosy pinks, invoking softness.

Call upon creatures displaying an air of grace and balance, such as giraffes and swans.

Place offerings of fans, gauze, hanging mobiles, flower arrangements, fruit, and beautiful and pleasing images.

Charge your altar with a mindful meditation in silence.

Affirmations

I surround myself with that which brings me calm.

I offer peace and harmony without letting it diminish my voice.

I choose the partners and collaborators who respect and honor my spirit.

I release myself from discordant relationships and environments.

Rituals

WEIGHING OPTIONS

Use this as an exercise to think things through. Conjure up a situation that requires you to weigh different sides or outcomes. Take a piece of paper and fold it into fourths. Keep the paper folded, and on one side, draw a shape or image that comes to mind when you think of one aspect of the situation. Connect the drawing to the other four sides and then carefully refold. Each consecutive day, trace the thread of where you left off on another side of the page without looking at what you drew before. On the fourth day, unfold your paper and see what its shapes have to tell you. Write it down.

BLEMISH

Meditate on that which you are trying to banish and move on from. Position yourself in front of a mirror so that your face is closely visible. Examine it. Choose a blemish, scar, or imperfection and name it after the object of your banishment. If your skin is flawless, look more closely and find something. Treat this discovery kindly over the next few weeks but be careful not to give it too much attention, for it may overstay its welcome. Note the way it changes in appearance day by day, week by week. By the time it melts away from your skin, you will notice a change. Draw it below, and give it a name.

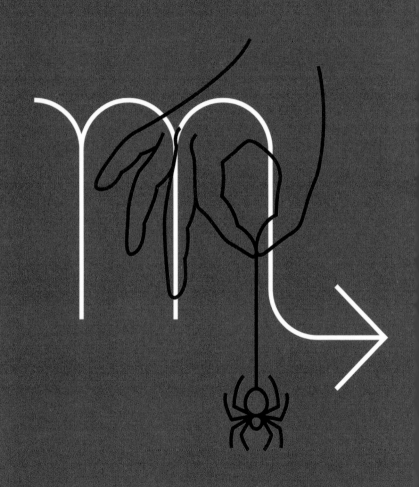

Scorpio

Eighth House of Transformation

There's a part of you that loves the dark side, but the truth is that intensity can apply itself to the highs and the lows, and every shade in-between. It's also true that feeling misunderstood can at times be central to your sense of self. This guardedness leads some to believe you are secretive, but it's really that this part of you experiences your emotions so intensely that being betrayed feels like a white-hot fury. You can also be deeply attuned to the emotional undercurrents of all interactions, with your radio antenna constantly making calculations, sending out signs and waves, in an attempt to echolocate those who just . . . get it. This is a magnetizing quality for people who also can sense you know something about going to the dark side and emerging all the wiser for having been reduced to ashes. You know what it means to heal on a deep level—and that it usually means drinking the poison in order to kill off what you no longer need in yourself. You're most at home in your power in these moments of deep transition, emotional intensity, and rebirth.

CONSTELLATION
The Scorpion

ELEMENT
Water

RULING PLANET
Pluto, Mars

QUALITY
Fixed

Moon Phase Horoscopes

NEW MOON *rest, recuperation, beginnings*

Sometimes it's necessary to absorb instead of act, to watch instead of do. Think of how quietly the sun can heat up the ground. Try to let your time move slowly. You don't have to know what you want and you don't have to take action if you're not ready. Try to keep your eyes open. It's good to be still, to ferment, to let things take slow root in your veins. It's okay to store your energy and dreams safely inside yourself, for now. You'll emerge brighter and more powerful than ever if you take this time to turn inward. Try sitting in your room at night with all the lights off. Feel the heavy blankness of the sky, close your eyes and see what shapes and feelings bubble to the surface of your mind. Try to draw them.

WAXING CRESCENT *energy, initiative, activation*

There's a part of you that lives for the beginnings of things. Think of snakes that shed their skin—the newness of bumping up against the world can make you feel vulnerable, but it can also make you feel alive. How can you use your powers of regeneration to let the waters of your darkest depths run clear again? Getting unstuck can come easily to you during this time when you apply your intensity to it. You can be highly attuned to these cycles of beginnings and endings, so be deliberate with what you are laying the foundation for. Practice doing something strangely methodical, like sorting leaves by their colors. What can it teach you about how to soften your gaze so you can focus more clearly?

FIRST QUARTER *balance, focus, commitment*

WAXING GIBBOUS *patience, cultivation, fine-tuning*

Sometimes you want to think of things as being all or nothing, to live at the polar extremes of feelings. It might be because inhabiting the middle space can feel murky. Try instead to think of yourself as a jigsaw puzzle or as an unsolvable riddle. It's hard to get a sense of balance and scale when you're constantly racing from one end of the emotional seesaw to the other. Your feelings can color everything you do and think. Try taking a piece of paper and writing down each decision you make each day. Assign each one a color that matches your current mood. After a few days, look back at how your feelings colored and influenced each decision you made. What insights want to emerge?

Patience can be hard earned, especially when you have blazing visions and a yearning to just inhabit the innermost core of a relationship or project as soon as it lifts off. But slowing down is sometimes the only way to prevent burning out. The middle path can be hard, the point in which the beginning seems so long ago and the future hasn't yet fully seemed to arrive. But there's a way to get your obsessive side to help your greatest potential, and that's by applying it to the painstaking details of whatever you're attempting to grow. Listen to songs that take their time to get started, read books that require you to focus on each word. Notice what they have to say to you about taking your own sweet time.

FULL MOON *completion, fulfillment, abundance*

You might find yourself getting freaked out by the big dreams and big plans that are showing themselves to you, that inhabit your deepest desires, and that finally feel just within reach. Remember that it's normal to want to run from the things we want the most—especially when they are just within reach. This is the place that your truest desires and strongest work and best dreams can come from. Let things be born in the chaos. You don't need things to make sense just yet. Check out a book on symbols from a library, study the shapes of moving clouds. Tap into the shadowy depths of your dreams, examine the soil they are rooted in. What do you want to let take hold? What shape will it take?

WANING GIBBOUS *review, reflection, introspection*

Consider the ways you haven't let yourself be destroyed by sadness, or loneliness, or by the world when it gets harsh. Honor the ways you've learned to breathe through it. Hold on to these warm glowing embers of the past and let them keep you strong and certain. There's a part of you that sometimes has a hard time letting go of people, of memories, of grief. It's a defense mechanism against ever being caught off guard, against ever being the most vulnerable. Instead, try asking yourself if it's possible to hold a memory without the weight of its emotion. Search for what is begging to be let go, then practice walking around without it and see how much lighter you feel in the world.

LAST QUARTER *discarding, amends, adjustment*

WANING CRESCENT *transition, healing, closure*

Try to let go of untying the broken knots in your core; try to love your whole complicated self. This is where your truest art generates. What would you need to get rid of to become the most blazing version of you? This is a time for endings, for completing a cycle. Look around for what has drained you and slowed you down. What is ready to become fuel because it is no longer needed? Who would you become if you made peace with a few of your demons? Sometimes our identity is so consumed with who we are not, that we forget who we actually are. Take time to watch something that is new to the world. Practice forming that kind of open and neutral curiosity, and notice how things begin to shift.

Everything around you and inside you is going to take on strange new shapes and vibrate with previously unseen colors. New cycles will form, taking over your dreams and the way you think. Even though this might squeeze old darknesses to the surface, try to remember all the good things you hold in your muscle memory. Stare at the outlines of oceans and mountains; study them. Do the things that feel indescribably urgent— things that make your heart flutter in your ribs. Do things for no other reason than to make yourself glow. Study images that show small, tentative growth, like the first glint of sunrise or a blade of grass poking through the snow. Search for that secret seed of relief in yourself.

Mood Phase Horoscopes

 **ROMANCE**

It's entirely possible that no one so intimately understands the dizzying depths and terrifying heights of love than this part of you. But it's that intensity that is your constant measuring stick, the barometer by which you measure all emotional weather. It's possible for this part of you to outwardly appear inscrutable, while underneath, endless currents are threatening to drag you under the water of your feelings. Naturally, this makes you ooze with strange desires, of which you reveal only the tip of the iceberg. When you find yourself turned inside out, unsure of which side is up or down, give yourself the space to breathe, to let the dust settle, and to let that dust transform itself through some strange alchemy into something productive.

FEAR

What is fear but a sign to pay attention to whatever lies underneath it? Sometimes it's better to be more curious about than frightened of fear and what it can reveal. Anything that forces you to peel back the surface and blink into the darkness underneath is a worthy endeavor. This is a part of you that isn't afraid to walk through fire, to drink from the poisoned chalice, to invite the monsters in your closet to a tea party. This is because there is always something to be learned, to be gained, by facing down and naming the things that scare you. Sometimes the lesson can be learned only through battle: that real transformation lies in forging yourself like a steel blade against the things you're cutting down.

● ● SUFFERING ● ● ●

Much in the same way that this part of you can easily access the darker emotions of the human psyche, pain is a space with which you are familiar, and at times, almost comfortable. Often you can bury yourself so deeply in a feeling that it can become hard to see when you are the architect of it. There's a point at which choosing to live inside pain becomes destructive, and at which you can become your own victim. The key is to remember the times in the past when you have emerged from pain reborn and resurrected as a new version of yourself. This side of you has a great capacity to heal the pain in others, which can be a great outlet for the bottled up intensity inside you.

REFLECTION

You'd think that because this part of you lives so easily in your feelings that it would be easy to reflect on your habits of being in the world. But it can be easy to get tunnel vision, which makes it hard to gain any perspective when you're in the middle of things. Something to consider is the fact that you have more in common emotionally with people than you'd like to think. There's a side of you that is constantly angling for control at the cost of realizing how it affects your relationships. The truth is that you'd rather people not witness the vulnerable parts of you because, in doing so, you give up some of your power. Stay hungry for the kinds of catharsis that reflection can offer you.

ANGER

There's a part of you that finds all feelings arousing, and anger is no exception. There's something about accessing all the musical notes of an emotion that you don't shy away from, and anger can clear-cut the forests of your relationships. Often, however, the anger that lashes out at others when you feel betrayed is anger you feel toward yourself for allowing yourself to become vulnerable. When you find yourself quickening to these lightning flashes, ask yourself what real evidence you have for these feelings. Be careful not to hold these sensations in your body, where they can store themselves like venom. Consider where else you could spend the currency of this energy. Think of the times you've truly forgiven in your life and what sweet release it brought you.

CHANGE

The problem with being able to reach such great heights of intensity in work, creativity, and relationships is the inevitable balancing act that occurs in order to create equilibrium. Much the same as with pain, this is a part of you that doesn't shy away from the depths, however dark they might be. This part of you knows that despair is often the doorway to realization and healing. Something must be shed before a new version can rise to the surface. This is a time to study the ancient process of alchemy, to understand on an atomic level how you can compost your sadness into something forged in light. The portals to transformation are often dark, lonely, and scary, but you are a true expert in navigating them.

 ## COMPASSION

Just because there's a part of you that is reluctant to give access to your inner world doesn't mean that you don't also take the weight of the world on your shoulders. The intensity this part of you can be prone to also applies itself to taking on the wounds of others. In the same way you are able to walk through darkness alone, you have the equal power to shine a light on the problems of others. This ability gives you the same courage that allows you to traverse the scarier paths in life, and your passionate nature gives you a determined quality. When you are able to unite compassion in the larger world with compassion for yourself and others, you become a lightning rod for transformation.

CONNECTION

It's hard when there's a part of you that is deeply allergic to small talk and that wants to peer deep inside someone's soul to the stuff that scares them. It's true that this side of yourself doesn't trust others that easily, but that is because you place value on the mutual exchange of vulnerability, of what it means to see and be seen. Loyalty is a kind of coded protection, which is why it is so important to you. This mystery on your part largely stems from an uncanny ability to sense the underlying energy and tides of any exchange or situation and then to adjust yourself accordingly by watching and listening. This in turn makes you an intense listener, tuning in on multiple frequencies to detect the hidden emotions underneath.

Altar

This season, use your altar as a shrine for processing
your deepest secrets.

Decorate your altar with black and blood reds,
invoking darkness and the underworld.

Call upon creatures of the night and those associated with
metamorphosis, such as snakes and moths.

Place offerings of bones and skulls, memento mori, keepsakes
and photos in memoriam, black leather and velvet, erotic images.

Charge your altar by writing and burning a list of things you
want to release during this time.

Affirmations

I honor the past while recognizing that which must die.

I commit to the transformations needed to break free of toxic cycles.

I do not shy away from difficult questions on my quest for truth.

I open myself to mystery and to finding power in the unknown.

Rituals

METAMORPHOSIS

Hold a funeral for your past selves, the ones that no longer serve you, the ones you owe nothing to. Sort through the dusty corners of your belongings for those items you're holding onto from past eras, that you can't bear to let go of but know in your heart that you should. Find a clean, comfortable place to surround yourself with these items. One by one, hold each item and say a prayer of gratitude and farewell. Sell or donate the things that can be reused or repurposed, transforming their power in new hands. Burn or sustainably discard the rest. Resist the urge to immediately fill the gaps: Sit with this raw, new self for a bit and breathe fresh air into those empty corners. Write a note of welcome to your new self.

_____

_____

_____

_____

_____

_____

_____

_____

_____

_____

LOOKING

Go and look at a living thing—a bush, a sleeping dog, a spider in its web—and keep looking until you feel you know something about it that you didn't know before. (If the thing you pick turns out to not be saying anything to you, try another one.) Now write a paragraph about it, trying to express that understanding in words. When you are done, you may have transformed your own image of the thing you looked at. Now look in the mirror and do it to yourself. Draw what you find.

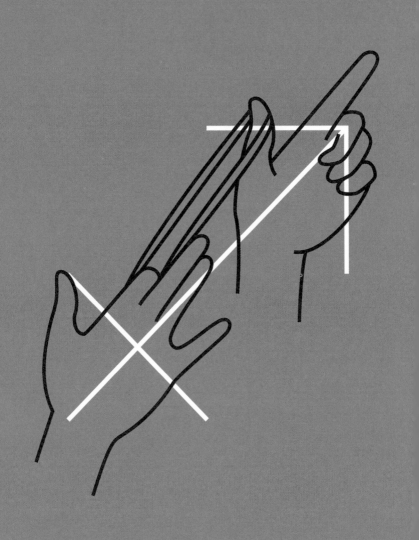

Sagittarius

NOVEMBER 23—DECEMBER 22
Ninth House of Exploration

There is a part of you that really doesn't have time for anything less than the truth, even if you pay the price of burning a bridge or two. This is because you are a seeker of facts, of meaning, and of information, which can prompt you to take off, at a moment's notice, to voraciously read every damn information placard at the museum. And if people can't keep up? There's no love lost because you'd likely rather do it on your own than wait around or follow someone else's itinerary. This goes for relationships, friendships, and going to the grocery store. Sometimes you don't need to dwell on the past, either; it can be more comfortable inhabiting a bird's-eye view from a safe distance.

CONSTELLATION
The Archer

ELEMENT
Fire

RULING PLANET
Jupiter

QUALITY
Mutable

Although some might accuse this mentality as cold or uncaring, that's far from true; you're innately curious about other people, as long as they can hold your attention. This side of you has a wicked sense of humor and makes you the first person your friends call when they want to take an impromptu road trip to some off-the-map destination. You're always seeking to live an inspired life and thrive on your freedom to do exactly that.

Moon Phase Horoscopes

NEW MOON *rest, recuperation, beginnings*

It can be easy to feel overwhelmed by your own dreams and desires, by your own bubbling self. It's okay to slow down until the swirling stops, until the sediment clears. Stay inside and ground yourself by cleaning out your closet or baking old family recipes. You'll find clarity but try to remember that it's okay to move quietly through your days. Reinvention and recalibration require you to get still in order to pinpoint your center of gravity—the art and music that truly moves you, the people who spark you to be your truest, fiercest self. If being still makes you itchy, try immersing yourself in the influences you feel most aligned with and inspired by, and cut out as much of the rest as you can.

WAXING CRESCENT *energy, initiative, activation*

You're right on the cusp of something huge, right on the edge of before and after. Try not to rush through the hours and minutes. Inhabit all this glowing anticipation, this not-knowing. Dig your heels into the shaky and wild present. What does reinvention mean to you? To invent is to come up with something entirely new, but to reinvent means you are composting the most fertile parts of yourself to mix the old with the new. When you're in this liminal in-between, it can be easy to keep adding things to carry with you out of fear or a sense of security. Try to rehearse the feelings and ways of thinking of this new you and ask yourself what in your former versions can most help you pave the path ahead.

FIRST QUARTER *balance, focus, commitment*

WAXING GIBBOUS *patience, cultivation, fine-tuning*

This is a time to call upon your inner reserves of boundless courage and strength in order to keep your momentum. There are the things you imagine will happen, and then there are the things that actually happen. How can you inhabit the middle space that allows for such upheavals? Sometimes a part of you can become so wedded to a particular vision that it can't see the other possibilities whizzing past. Practice tuning your antennae into other ways of seeing. It's possible to keep your vision fixed on a distant dot while also being fluid with how you get there. Read choose-your-own-adventure stories; draw maps and trace all the different possible routes to get from one place to another.

What if you were given an object that you didn't know how to use? Sometimes we become aware of something's significance only incrementally, as though its powers can't be unleashed all at once. Think of all the things you might have found a magical use for if only you had allowed its powers to unfold when you were ready to see them. Try putting a sponge or a tightly wound root in a bowl of water. Notice how long it takes to let go, to expand and unfurl to its full capacity. This is how long it might take for you to take full advantage of your own expanding and of the things the currently appear in your life like dense stones but which secretly house the power to make you grow in unexpected directions.

FULL MOON *completion, fulfillment, abundance*

WANING GIBBOUS *review, reflection, introspection*

Be alert to any buzzing sensations in your brain, any strange vibrations on the wind. There is a part of you that experiences the world through your intellect rather than through your feelings. What symbols, colors, music, and art can you attune yourself to right now in order to spark a sense of your own intuition? Some of what you notice might confuse you, offering up more questions than answers. Record the questions as they occur to you and keep them in a secret place. Revisit them during the next full moon, and write down what messages they've revealed to you since then. Sometimes it takes time to decode the answers and to realize that perhaps you just weren't ready to see them before this moment.

Dig deep into the truth of who you are, who you want to be, and who you've been. There are so many versions of you that live inside your skin, and sometimes they don't always listen to each other. There is wisdom that already lives in your skin, that's already buried deep in your bones. It is an accumulation of the wisdom of all the yous—past, present, and future. Listen to them closely. It's good to review who's on your internal committee every so often, to hear out their conflicts and see who's been holding the microphone for too long. Write a one-act screenplay of all your yous debating a current conflict. Name them, hear them out, write their back stories, and examine which ones are serving your best interest.

LAST QUARTER *discarding, amends, adjustment*

WANING CRESCENT *transition, healing, closure*

There's a part of you that doesn't mind the ending of things, since endings are a harbinger of something bright and new peeking over the horizon. There's merit to being able to make a clean break with the things that have done the work they came to do. Look at the sea and the stars in the night sky and then turn and look into yourself for the answers you now crave. Travel somewhere far enough that the air smells new and the light looks different. Leave the things you need to discard in the ground there. Travel somewhere that makes you understand what it means to go home, even if it's just to a new tree or getting lost in the landscape of a book. How have your perspectives shifted?

You might feel dazzled by the sensation that casting off old ways of being can conjure. A new incarnation of you can emerge, shimmering like a mirage. Think about babies, about fools, about a time when you knew nothing and had everything to learn. Try to remember what it's like to inhabit that space, to soak up sensations. When your world is reborn, the realest thing can be knowing how much you don't yet know. While that sense of not knowing can terrify some people, there's a part of you that relishes an embarkation point into the unknown future. There are no boundaries here, only possibilities to examine. Try writing a list of all the things you don't yet know or of all the things you've been wrong about.

Mood Phase Horoscopes

 **ROMANCE**

Love is a two-way street, and it demands a mutual respect when it comes to space, trust, and independence. There's a part of you that desires both the provocation of a partner yet deeply requires the freedom to change both yourself and your plans at a moment's notice. This can create a tension between what you feel compelled to do versus what you feel obligated to do, and the minute this part of you sniffs out a sense of obligation, it would rather wander off somewhere else. The challenge for this part of you is to experience someone else's desires as something to be intellectually curious about rather than caged in by. Give yourself the gift of carving out your own space within the boundaries of someone else's love.

REFLECTION

It's not that there's a part of you that's scared of reflection, it's that you're already pretty sure you know the how and why of everything you've gone through the moment it's happened. Consider allowing yourself some time and distance to revisit patterns and memories. This part of you experiences reflection through an intellectual lens rather than an emotional one. One thing to practice is writing down your experience of an event after it happens and then revisiting it after some time has passed. Be open to what it has to teach you—can you apply your open-mindedness to your own sense of self? Consider the times you've been wrong in the past: How did that revelation change your sense of what you think you know versus what you actually know?

COMPASSION

One of the facets of true compassion is an acknowledgment that things can be complicated, difficult, and contradictory. This part of you, however, is always hunting for the shortest path to the bluntest truth. It can be difficult for you to dwell on the past, and while this might look like a good thing on the surface, it can also mean you are quick to forget the feelings that accompanied it. Moving on with such lightning speed means you don't get to use the muscles that are flexed when compassion stretches you by forcing you to dwell on someone else's pain. This part of you believes that blunt truth is the highest compliment, but remember that not everyone can swallow the truth. How can you use your intellect to take on another's perspective that might differ from your own?

CONNECTION

This part of you has such a strong sense of self that you can't stand anyone assuming they know you when they don't. Conversely, you refuse to hide behind a persona or alter yourself to please anyone. There's a part of you that thrives on being surrounded by other curious people, and when you're at ease, your optimism can flow freely. Your search for truth means that you don't have time for people who waste it by obfuscating, and rather than make a big deal about it, you're likely to walk away instead. Try listening rather than reacting if someone has the facts wrong. This means that you are nearly impossible to manipulate, but it also means that you can be reckless with others' feelings. Use your objectivity to try to empathize with the way your words can affect people.

CHANGE

This is a part of you that is always willing to start from zero and to be a blank slate for the world to write its wisdom on. This instills in you a deep need for traveling, experiencing, and exploring, and your innate curiosity means you're not one to run from whatever strong situations you might find yourself in. To be a true seeker means constantly admitting what you don't already know, and the only time you trip yourself up is when you assume you that you do know. When you feel yourself going rigid in your worldviews, think back to a time when learning something left you utterly humbled and remember that you will always have the capacity to empty yourself out in order to be transformed.

WORK

The key for this part of you is to find a way not to see work as work. Try to move toward projects where you are the creator of ideas and experiences, the big-picture thinker, rather than the checker of details or the producer of actual, tangible things. You work best when allowed to follow the zigzagging line of your own interests, freedom, and passions, when you can find a natural outlet for your restlessness. Anything that expands your mind or understanding of the world will light you up, and cause you to blaze uncharted paths without needing to worry about the nitty-gritty. Look for situations that encourage by saying "Yes, try that" rather than telling you what not to do.

ACTION

This is a part of you that has so many ideas, so many lighbulbs exploding from the weight of your mental and philosophical calculations. But it can be easy to grow bored by the sometimes slow and methodical tasks of seeing an idea to fruition, or adhering to someone else's timeline. Take care to get out of your head and intellect every so often in order to apply the abstract to the concrete, to make something where there used to be nothing. How can you keep your flames burning long enough to bring your ideas to fruition? Give yourself tangible reminders of what you've set out to do, such as setting alarms with one-word reminders to go off at different times throughout the day.

STAGNATION

While for some people getting stuck means never getting off the couch, for this part of you it means the inability to focus, or flitting from one thing to the next without ever fully committing. But no matter how far you travel or how many books you read, you will always return to yourself. And if that self makes you feel antsy, it's time to create some sparks that can carry you through the doldrums. Assign yourself a project that explores the roots of this stuckness—what have you grown bored of? What in your life needs to be pruned back to its essentials? Make a collage with the words and colors that give shape and definition to where you're at and where you're headed.

Altar

This season, use your altar as a bridge to your independence.

Decorate your altar with violet and indigo, invoking the cosmos.

Call upon migratory creatures and beasts of long-distance racing and chasing, such as wolves and geese.

Place offerings of atlases, compasses, telescopes, constellation maps, astronomical equipment, books, airplanes, images of the places you want to go.

Charge your altar by taking in a deep breath and then laughing, howling, or exhaling into the night sky.

Affirmations

I hold wonder in the universe and revel in its vastness.

I explore uncharted paths and seek perspectives that are beyond my scope.

I see the difference between releasing what ties me down and running away from what I must face.

I expand and evolve my mind and spirit in order to be free.

Rituals

ANIMAL CARTOGRAPHY

The next time you are in an unfamiliar place, see if you can unlearn
the ways you approach these spaces, like when you gloss over the mundane. Take note of your environment the way an animal might: tracing
perimeters, ears wide and scanning, muzzle pointed like a divining
wand. Observe the plants, bugs, birds, gravel, dirt, trash, shadows,
and silhouettes. Run your hands over surfaces. Feel the velocity of
passing people in your bones. If there are structures, read any/all signs
and plaques; look at the building material. What does it smell like, what
are the ambient sounds, what is the density of the air? How old is it?
What layers can you unearth just by looking? If you were placed here
again blindfolded, would you be able to recognize it? Record what you
learned below.

JOLT

Take a walk somewhere you traverse frequently, an area so familiar it registers as unremarkable. Make an effort to observe things you may have never noticed before, to tune your senses to the sounds, smells, light, shadows, and movements. Turn off the part of your brain that wants to judge, decide, plan ahead. Let yourself wander intuitively, as if an invisible thread is gently leading you, but watch out for traffic. At some point, something unfamiliar will deliver a jolt to your core. Observe what that something is. In the space below, intuitively draw an abstract shape to represent your experience, and below it, quickly write three words that come to mind. Visit it every day until its message reveals itself.

Capricorn

There are people who get things done, and then there are people who *Get. Things. Done.* And you are one of those people, but you certainly already knew that. What most people don't often realize at first is the metric ton of creative energy you harbor under your calm, cool demeanor. That's probably because what is a creative struggle for most people is determined ambition on your part. You won't attempt a single thing you don't already know the outcome of, whether that's romantically, professionally, or creatively. You've also learned that you really can't rely on anyone but yourself to get things done to your level of satisfaction. It may not look glamorous, but it's the kind of seamless work that everyone else takes for granted. It also means you're often the bearer of buckets of cold water to throw on other people's lofty, unlikely dreams. The thing to remember is that the same level of drive doesn't appeal or apply to everyone. No one's ever going to get too mad at you, however, because you are also one of the funniest people alive. Sometimes it just takes a while for you to let your stoic guard down.

CONSTELLATION
The Sea-Goat

ELEMENT
Earth

RULING PLANET
Saturn

QUALITY
Cardinal

Moon Phase Horoscopes

NEW MOON *rest, recuperation, beginnings*

Who are you when you're not doing, not thinking, not worrying? Consider the notion that you can maximize your powers while sitting still, while clearing your mind, or while letting your restless hands sit in your lap. It's the quiet spaces that can fortify you and carve themselves out to be filled again. If you're constantly busy, you can never completely empty yourself out in order to be renewed. Learning how to sit with nothing can also build your stamina to do the hardest work, like an extra arm you can use when you're at capacity. Set aside time each day to gaze at something that makes you feel peacefully empty, like a dull gray stone or an empty parking lot. What does stillness have to teach you?

WAXING CRESCENT *energy, initiative, activation*

Rather than grope blindly for the resources you believe you need to begin something, contemplate the notion that everything you need is within your immediate grasp. How can the structure you are working within inform the very thing you are creating? Whether it's for work or love or friendship or creativity, look closely at the foundations you are pouring. While they're not set in stone just yet, the intention you set at the beginning will influence the outcome in ways you may not anticipate. For this reason, take care to make yourself available to forces that run deeper than the ones you can merely see or touch. Make a list of the things you need in order to call the thing you want into existence both tangible and intangible.

FIRST QUARTER *balance, focus, commitment*

Even if you can't feel your feet on the ground, you're still you. You're still all the pieces all the time. You can change like the winds. You can wax and wane like the moon. Try to be kind to the parts of yourself you don't like. Try to be kind to the sad and vulnerable part of you. There's a part of you that would like to keep a safe distance from things that might cause you pain, might knock you off kilter, might divert you from the task at hand. But sometimes the things and moods you encounter on the winding trails alongside you hold the key to your becoming; they have something that will allow you to access the dormant parts of you that have been yearning to be heard. Get quiet and listen.

WAXING GIBBOUS *patience, cultivation, fine-tuning*

So often we look to the world around us to reflect back clues about who we are supposed to be. But it's worth thinking about the smallest and quietest decisions you constantly make that craft you into the person you are molding into, that shape the life you're building. Think back to some of your hardest-won wisdom. What dreams have you postponed because you don't feel as though you've done the work to step into them yet? The problem is that putting dreams off until you feel you've mastered each step means you miss out on the messy truths that come with living, the secret badges of honor that come from making the mistakes that reroute you along paths you would never have ventured otherwise.

FULL MOON *completion, fulfillment, abundance*

Sometimes you'll to have to trust your heart more than your own eyes; you'll have to pay attention to the goosebumps on your skin. Close your eyes, relax into these sensations, and practice seeing while sightless. This can be hard to do, especially if you are accustomed to trusting only what tangible things can tell you. What are the sensations in your body trying to tell you? What are the unseen energies you glance through every day, and how might they influence you more than you realize? The things you dream while you sleep are also a part of you, and they're worth writing down in order to notice what subconscious worries and yearnings are driving your decisions under the surface during your waking hours.

WANING GIBBOUS *review, reflection, introspection*

Try watching people when they're talking and count the pauses between their sentences. It's going to freak you out a little, being this observant. Try not to judge what you notice. Do your best to peer below the surface. What other senses can you observe with? The unspoken messages you encounter during this time have hidden data embedded in their silences. Are there any particular illusions about people, projects, or yourself that you've been clinging to despite contrary evidence about their true nature? Now is a time for noting the discrepancies, for seeing what strange pathways they illuminate toward a different narrative than you might have considered. Write out all the possible different options.

LAST QUARTER *discarding, amends, adjustment*

WANING CRESCENT *transition, healing, closure*

Do what you can to finally let go of the things in your life that make your mouth taste bitter when you think about them. Throw them in the churning ocean or burn them in a bonfire or just list them in a notebook for another time, for when you're ready. Prepare yourself for lighter, unencumbered days. There's a part of you that deeply understands the technical side of these cycles, of shredding documents and cleaning out your desk drawer. Yet it's important to recognize the emotional resonance you attach to these accumulations, like pebbles at the bottom of a river that bruise your feet when you step on them. Practice creating a small ritual of release and feel the sweet relief of ridding yourself of their weight.

Transitions require a willingness to relinquish power over the past while admitting uncertainty about the future. This can be hard if you are constantly searching for equilibrium, but remember that you are the source of your own restoration. The external world need not weigh in on how you should navigate the shifting sands of change. There's no one way to master the in-between; there's only recognition of what is occurring and the ability to inhabit that space without chomping at the bit. This is a time to contemplate how the tiniest pebbles you drop in the water right now will reverberate into the future, so take some time trying out different sizes, shapes, and textures in order to observe the kinds of waves they make.

Mood Phase Horoscopes

REFLECTION

There's a part of you that relishes closing the book on an experience after it's over and moving on to what's next. There can be a serious quality to you that screws up its face when forced to reflect on the past and the things you can no longer change, because you'd rather be looking ahead to a future you can prepare for. Yet there's wisdom to be gained by looking backward sometimes, at noting the ways you've learned to navigate the complexities of the world. Allow yourself to trace the current through-lines of your life back to their origins, if only as a reminder that when you feel worry about beginning something again, you're a quick learner who has the distinct capacity to adapt to whatever life hands you.

COMPASSION

What does it mean to give space to the notion that some circumstances can't be controlled, no matter how much you wish they could be? While there's a part of you that wishes it could walk away rather than deal in complexity, there's a way to use your pragmatism for its greatest good. This means that you have the power to take the concrete steps to make things better for others when they can't. You have the secret skill of being able to divorce your feelings from the task at hand. By the same token, it's normal to allow yourself to go a little soft around the edges when you see someone in pain, to offer yourself up as a grounded center for someone to lean their entire being against.

WORK

There's a part of you whose sense of identity is closely tied to the work you do. Work can be a largely unemotional thing, able to be quantified and measured. This part of you has a quiet and tenacious determination that makes it look as if you're not even breaking a sweat over things that would make anyone else burst into tears. The way you move through the world is a reflection of how you approach work: with confidence and discipline. Try to remember, though, that you can apply this same determination to other parts of your life that feel less controllable yet need it—and that it can be good to bask in the unknowable outcome every now and then.

 ## CONNECTION

This is a part of you that can be a tough nut to crack. While you can be patient with those you love, you can be so self-reliant that no one can find a way to access your interiority. But being able to witness someone's inner self is the most profound gift you can give another. Remember that although you are resourceful, there are people around you who would love to be your resource as well. Allowing them to do so might require you to bend in a way that feels a little unnatural, but that can be a good thing. You have strong opinions built on solid reasoning, and this gives you a solid, steady magnetism that naturally brings the people who resonate to you.

 **ROMANCE**

Once you grant access past your defense fortresses, the people you let in are your people for life. This is a part of you that applies the same tenacity to your relationships as it does to your work and creative projects. One might even catch a glimpse of something that looks like devotion on your face when you're surrounded by the people who have earned your trust. You are interested only in the ties that are built to endure and weather the storms of life. This gives you an intuition for anyone who isn't rooted in their own sincerity. Remember that it's okay to let your guard down, sometimes, so that you can be pleasantly surprised by who the world sends sailing through your gates.

 **CHANGE**

Shifting gears can be hard for this part of you. You revel in the slow building of something over time that can endure, and it can be hard to say goodbye and make way for something new and uncertain to arrive. Your inner compass is often pointed toward pessimism, scanning the horizon for all the possible things that might go wrong. Remember in these moments that your self-reliance has gotten you past so many obstacles and that your perseverance in straddling a transition means the sailing often appears smoother than it does for others. It's okay to take a moment and inhabit an unknown space, waiting to be filled. Close your eyes for just a minute and fall into all that expansive space waiting to meet you.

ACTION

Who are you when you're not in motion? Remember that it's okay to sink into the journey as well—because it's there that you truly learn the things you came to learn anyway. Some of your efficiency is a defense against uncertainty, a way to take the surest route where you can see everything around you unfold. You like to be in charge, but consider the fact that one of the underused parts of you is the one that can relinquish control and trust others to get things done. Practice letting go of this sense of responsibility sometimes. But in order to survive, you must know yourself on all counts, and knowing who you are when you need other people is a good version of yourself to know.

SUFFERING

Thanks to your antennae always being tuned to the weight of the world and your responsibilities in it, it can be easy to become bogged down by the heaviness that entails. Even though your identity can be that wrapped up in this sense of duty, if you keep piling on weight, you might drown. At the same time, you can't be rushed out of these moods; this part of you needs to learn how to find relief and rely on others. One outlet you can look toward is humor—how can you create something relatable and amusing out of this constant access to heaviness? Write jokes, draw comics, go to weird stand-up nights and laugh until you cry. No one understands better than you the intersection of tragedy and comedy.

Altar

This season, use your altar as a pedestal for all that you have worked hard for.

Decorate your altar with steely grays, invoking the highest mountains.

Call upon the mountain goat and other beasts of wisdom, agility, and diligence.

Place offerings of ribbons and trophies, cityscapes, abacuses and calculators, hourglasses and clocks, aspirational images, images of people you admire.

Charge your altar with a mental visualization of your best potential self.

Affirmations

I manifest the blueprints for reaching my greatest potential.

I draw the boundaries needed to protect my time and energy.

I challenge myself to be better and wiser every day.

I remind myself that I am more than what I achieve and accomplish.

Rituals

SACRED SPACE

For this ritual, you should try something new for a period of time, something you've been wanting to try that you've avoided thus far because you feel wobbly about it or never quite prepared. Here's the catch: You are to do this for you and only you. For some, this sacred space comes easy; for others, not so much. You may tell one or two close confidantes about this new practice, and you may keep a private journal, but you are not to document it in any way publicly; there's no need for validation. Seek a practice that makes you feel good and blanket yourself in the sacred spirit of it. After a month, see if you notice any changes from incorporating this practice, and see if you can integrate them into the rest of your life. Record what you learned below

THE SHAPE OF CHAOS

Walk around your home and collect ten small objects with different personalities that you use for different things. Scatter them on a flat surface. Fiddle with the objects, moving them into geometries or clusters. Tease them into shapes and architectures. See if you can detect a structural backbone to the set. Notice if the surface you are arranging them on lends a voice. Keep going until you arrive at a conclusion that feels as if the objects have transcended themselves and have something unified and complete. What purpose might it serve? What new ideas or ways of thinking might it offer a bridge to? Diagram the process below.

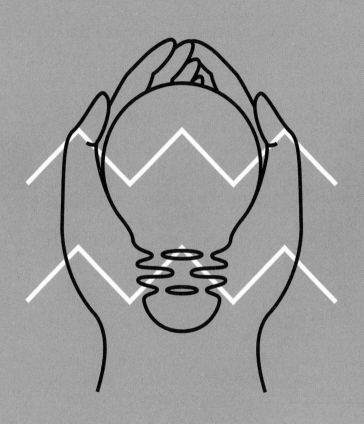

Aquarius

Eleventh House of Humanity

Sometimes we can tune into different frequencies of being: feeling, thinking, just existing. There's a part of you that finds relief in taking the long view, the bird's-eye view. This stance allows you to think about yourself from the angle of encompassing humanity rather than the daily frictions of what it means to be you in your own little world. This is a time to investigate what being free truly means to you. What could you create or invent that could push the boundaries of existence as you know it? Take advantage of being able to glimpse the possibilities of the future, unattached to it. There's a balance to be struck, though, between aloof detachment and emotional investment, and that balance can be tricky to navigate when you are more comfortable in your thinking mind. Although distance can allow you to operate without being subject to the moods that accompany feelings, you can run the risk of becoming too fixated on maintaining this distance. How can you integrate these different selves to produce your most innovative work in the world?

CONSTELLATION
The Water Bearer

ELEMENT
Air

RULING PLANET
Uranus

QUALITY
Fixed

Moon Phase Horoscopes

NEW MOON *rest, recuperation, beginnings*

This is a time to get centered, and find the small, still orb inside you that lights your path ahead. Wake up to watch the sky turn pink; turn off the lights and watch the moon change; and see what they both have to tell you. Use this moment for your inborn curiosity to find a way to observe your mind in the midst of all this stillness. What new colors do you see around you? What sounds do you hear behind the hum of the universe? What extremes were you previously blind to that you can now combine into some new rare element? Remember that slowing down can allow you the precious space to discover new realms inside yourself. Make a weird electronic song of all the new sounds filling up inside you.

WAXING CRESCENT *energy, initiative, activation*

Your thoughts are going to feel so clear; you're going to be able to see far enough to believe in your own future, to see all the places you'll go and the people you'll love. Remember that you can create what you don't yet know exists. You can build the things that you need that don't yet have names. Write down as many words to describe these desires as you can think of: their shapes and feelings. Tap into the energy in your beating heart and the twitchiness of your fingers. Look for your reflection in windows and puddles and mirrors. See what that reflection is trying to tell you when you're caught off guard. Don't ever doubt your sweet heart. Do the hard work and sit still with the hard thoughts.

FIRST QUARTER *balance, focus, commitment*

Stay open to every eerie possibility, every unlit door, every disguised gift. Be ready to surprise yourself: This is how you get stronger and stranger. This the place that your truest desires and strongest work and best dreams can come from. Things don't have to try to make sense right now; just let them be born in the chaos and trust that you will know the shape to mold them into from there. Pay close attention to the pinches and flashes of happiness that flare up inside you, all vibrant and brimming. This is a time for tending to you above all else. Think back to the times you've met someone or received something without yet knowing the profound impact it would have on you. Practice staying in that space of openness.

WAXING GIBBOUS *patience, cultivation, fine-tuning*

This is a time for testing out your newfound strengths and for growing in strange new directions. Try to hold your hand; try to steady your wobbly legs. You might feel as if you're stitched together out of so many fabrics filled with wild colors and feelings, and everything might feel as if it's full of weird riddles for which the solution is just out of reach. The universe wants to see what you can do when you get frustrated; it wants to give you space to prove something to yourself. Don't get stuck. You've been here before, and those practices have sharpened your teeth and made you stronger. Let your thoughts move in weird patterns, like spirals or trapezoids. What can these new ways of thinking show you?

FULL MOON *completion, fulfillment, abundance*

WANING GIBBOUS *review, reflection, introspection*

You're gonna start to get a little itch in your heart. You might be yearning for a life you're not quite living yet, a life you've only glimpsed in your dreams at night like reverse déjà vu. It might make you feel a little antsy and weak, but only if you let it. It can also be a map, a road, a fire burning bright in the distance. What have you done in the past when you're all out of magic? Make a list of all the sparks that ignite you, whether they're people or songs or photographs. What balm can you apply to this spiritual itch to keep your course steady, your gaze focused? Think of all the times you've gotten from point to point in your life, sometimes fast and sometimes slow. Let your former selves lead the way.

You might feel electricity in the air, a humming in your head, or a buzzing in your bones that only you can perceive. Think of it as a secret message. The doors you open will be the ones you need to walk through. If you feel overwhelmed, try to remember that you alone get to choose what you spend your energy focusing on. Let these new feelings fill you with new colors. Let them take root in your bones. Let them show you how to live on a different frequency. If you sit very still, you can catch a glimpse of the future and of the moments adding up to something bright and looming. How can you make sure you are ready to meet it? Let this glimpse sharpen your focus and try not to get distracted.

LAST QUARTER *discarding, amends, adjustment*

You might start to see your hard work begin to take shape; you might start to see what all your doubts have been for. If you're willing to turn your gaze and focus outward, away from your brain, you'll be rewarded. It's okay to dream outside the lines of your life and see what your weird and tangled brain conjures up. This is a time to give space to your own weird unspoken desires that you've been too scared to say out loud to yourself. Let them breathe; give them some water. It's okay if you need to spend your days catching your balance again. It's okay if you need to spend your days honoring the stillness in your heart and the uncertainties that dot your path. Remember that you've been here before.

WANING CRESCENT *transition, healing, closure*

This time can be full of wonder, full of fuzzy feelings that you can't even name because they are so new and weird. Your brain might feel strange this month, like your dreams have changed shape and color, like your insides are made of cotton, like whole new kinds of feelings are sprouting in your heart. Don't overthink the ways you are growing right now. Don't second-guess them. Just let them light up your world and guide you where you need to go. Walk down different streets to work; open your windows at night to let the moon in. This is a time for shaking free of some of your patterns and beliefs, for seeing what sticks to you like a magnet, and for throwing what doesn't into the garbage can.

Mood Phase Horoscopes

 **ROMANCE**

Practice the art of giving someone the same sharp attention and focus you give to your ideas and creative pursuits. When you find yourself in this space, get around this fickleness by splitting your attention between other forms of self-expression—record that experimental album, paint a self-portrait of all the versions of yourself, cook something using only the ingredients you have on hand. When you spread yourself around, oddly enough, you have the release to focus on your scattered feelings. Use that newfound focus to overcome the challenge of being present with a single person. Remember that people have just as much to show you as books or museums. Allow yourself to be captivated and curious by someone and to witness their becoming.

CONNECTION

So much of the tension within friendships can come from whether or not we feel seen and whether we can share a mutual vulnerability and trust. Practice the art of being fully present with whoever is in your company, of taking it all in and refracting back the complexity you notice through your own light. This is a part of you that can by turns come off as aloof and intense, so remember to thank your friends for the dynamism they provide you and the ways they fill you up. People are endless sources of constant change and variables, and there's a part of you that can find these nuances endlessly fascinating. Choose to surround yourself with the people who force growth in you.

REFLECTION

Remembering is how we learn and digest information and experiences. Be careful not to fool yourself into believing that just because you can see the pattern or issue clearly, you know what caused it or how to prevent repeating yourself in the future. Your confidence is your superpower, but if the foundational supports grow weak, an unfamiliar doubt might begin to creep in. The way to keep your belief in yourself and your actions strong is to allow yourself time to look backward and connect what you do with what you feel. Practice the art of taking time at the end of every day or week to reflect on your experiences both small and large, noticing the way they've settled into the fabric of your being.

STAGNATION

Getting unstuck can mean getting comfortable with the notion that you may not have all the answers and data at your disposal, that some things might remain cloudy until you follow your gut. Rather than isolate yourself in these moments, turn toward the people who can read you best and who can lovingly nudge you out of your aloofness. Sometimes you can't easily spot that your stuckness is rooted in a fear from the past that has followed you into your future. In order to take it all in, think deeply about what contradictions are up for review and how you might see more clearly any of those shimmering mirages for what they are to walk through them to the truth. Try to remember the times you've gotten unstuck in the past.

FEAR

There comes a point at which your fixed nature serves only to keep you rooted in a place of distant remove while everything else passes you by. Consequently, when you're not attuned with the currents of life, you can feel unnoticed, which shakes your sense of self to its very core. This is a part of you that's not afraid to suffer or sacrifice if that's the correct path, but remember that before anyone else, you provide the torch that lights up your contributions to the world. This may mean stepping into a new version of you, of inhabiting it and trying it on before anyone can see it. Try rehearsing these feelings as though they are already true.

ANGER

There's a part of you that would like to believe you're not prone to the same range of emotions as other human beings, that you've mastered control over them, and that can turn them on and off like a faucet. If you're not careful, the feelings you're squelching will seep out in other ways, perhaps in a passive aggressive way, which can act like a silent but deadly poisonous gas. Think back to instances when you've had conflict with others and write a list of the resolutions that came from clearing the air. Remember that strange sense of relief, rehearse it, and call upon it the next time you need to express your anger. Imagine your anger as something to be cleaned out, released, and cleared.

STRENGTH

Applying your brand of inquisitiveness and cerebral intellect to the world around you lets you occupy a space in which your insights aren't necessarily bogged down by your feelings about them. Let it be a reminder to you that this sense of restlessness can keep moving you forward, to make it so that you're unlikely to get bogged down with the heavy things that you no longer need or serve your greatest visions. Whatever it is you are working toward, create a list of all the seen and unseen influences propelling it into being. Keep adding to it. Consider the notion that perhaps it's not the answers you seek but, rather, what you create that can reveal yourself to you.

COMPASSION

While many people feel compassion for humanity, our emotions can cause reactions that don't allow for a clear, long view of the breadth and scope of what it means to be a human. This part of you has an ability to see clearly the larger forces at work in shaping how humanity communicates, connects, and causes one another to suffer, and your intellect allows you to come up with innovations and solutions that may not occur to those who are led by their feelings. When extending that same compassion to those closest to you, however, remember that sometimes listening, rather than solving, is the compassionate muscle to use. Practice reflecting back to people what you hear them saying in a new way.

Altar

This season, use your altar to remind you of your place in the grand scheme of the universe.

Decorate your altar with electric sky blues, invoking the future.

Call upon birds with high perches and other unusual and intelligent creatures.

Place renderings of punk and anarchist galaxies and nebulas, neon, abstract art, cacti, images of science and innovation.

Complete your altar by drafting a personal and political manifesto.

Affirmations

I offer my uniqueness as a gift to the collective.

I synthesize the unexpected from eclectic sources.

I rebel against oppressive forces and structures.

I choose to be an active participant in securing the future of humanity.

Rituals

COMMON THREAD

Obtain two spools of thread of different colors that will stand out against your environment. Choose a close friend and give one of the spools to them. Visit a local public space together, choosing one that is not too big but not too small. Stand in the middle, divide the area into equal halves, and then flip a coin to assign each half to one of you. Part ways and explore your respective halves separately for a healthy stretch of time (however long you choose). Every time something catches your eye or makes you look closer, tie a small bow on it with your colored thread; your friend should do the same. At the end of your exploration, meet back in the middle. Visit each other's respective halves and find all your friend's thread markers, removing each one and making a note of where it was. What is the common thread? Record what you learned below.

VESSELS

This month, try to have nontrivial conversations with two people, one older and one younger. They can be family, friends, neighbors, or strangers. A significant age gap in either direction is ideal; see if you can also seek out people whose lives are as different from yours as possible. Suspend your judgment and be a vessel for their words, thoughts, and experiences. What can you learn from them? What wisdom can be gleaned from differences in perspective? What unconscious biases do you notice rearing their heads, making you flinch? What new compassions can you breed? Draw their portraits below, and record what they taught you.

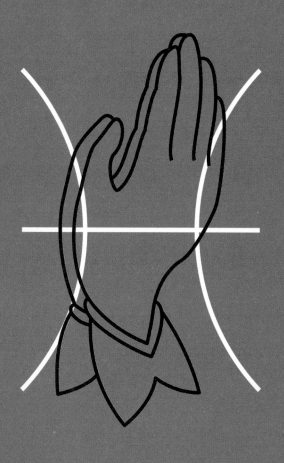

Pisces

Imagine being born into the weightless space of water. How would you move through the world, what sort of heightened sensitivities would you develop? This part of you is designed for the life of dreams, of hovering in between worlds. It allows you to gaze past the tangible and tap into shifting energies. How can you access what lies below the surface without using it for escape when you feel overwhelmed? Your abilities have something to tell you about receptivity, which can be a gift as well as a danger. You can let yourself sink into an inner wisdom, a place where your gut will always lead you to the right place. When you realize that only you have the answers you seek, you'll stop turning to people who just want to rescue you from the watery depths. In turn, your compassionate and wise nature can be a beacon for partnerships of all kinds. How can you prepare yourself by marking the boundaries you need? Remember that the art of solitude can also help you define your blurry edges. This part of you blooms when you express yourself through the art you create and the relationships you cultivate.

CONSTELLATION
The Fish

ELEMENT
Water

RULING PLANET
Neptune, Jupiter

QUALITY
Mutable

Moon Phase Horoscopes

NEW MOON *rest, recuperation, beginnings*

WAXING CRESCENT *energy, initiative, activation*

You can find things to fill up the parts of yourself that feel neglected, you can soothe the parts of you that are aching, and you can mend the things that are torn. The private, watery world that you inhabit can feel calm, kind, soothing, and restful. This is a time when the stormy seas can subside, when the sharp voices in your head can turn into gentle whispers, and when the air stays still and you can hear the quiet hum of the universe behind it. Let yourself inhabit this solidness; let yourself sink into the soft, firm earth for once. Try expanding in such a way that you can notice where you end and other people or places begin. Remember that you can always come back to this still center of existing.

This is a time for weeding and watering your wild inner landscape, for paying close attention to the flashes of happiness that flare up inside you, all vibrant and brimming. This is a time for tending to you above all else. Don't wait for anyone to tell you how to live your life. You don't owe anybody anything other than to be your truest self. Stay up until dawn writing weird poetry or walk down the quiet streets in your town under buzzing streetlights. Fill yourself up with all this strange beauty and let it do things to your heart. Make a list of all the things you are planting there, and next to the entries write all the ways you can coax them to grow. Remember that only you have access to the still center that guides you.

FIRST QUARTER *balance, focus, commitment*

WAXING GIBBOUS *patience, cultivation, fine-tuning*

Try not to hold yourself back from your impulses toward vulnerability. Try not to doubt your open heart or your warm faith in yourself. You already know the best things about yourself, even if the world tries to cram you with doubt. You know which way your heart naturally turns, toward what's right and true. Trust these urges. Feed them with bravery. It might make your emotional muscles ache, but in a way that shows that you are getting stronger and braver. Draw a comic of yourself in your most courageous moments. Draw the antagonists and evil villains you slay, even if they were just thoughts, feelings, or strangers on the bus. How can seeing a different perspective of yourself show you something new and true?

You'll feel the world shifting in waves around you during this time, as if you're floating at sea or standing on a moving train. It can be hard to get your bearings when you've got places to go, but try to let this uncertainty guide your reactions. Lean into the swells and relax into this wobbliness. Let yourself be surprised at what emerges. Something in you is going to begin to spark and glow; your veins are going to start coursing with a wild and unfamiliar energy. The power you're going to begin to realize you have over your own life might startle you and scare you. Just try to believe in your own weirdness, even when your own wobbly thoughts are still taking shape. Try not to doubt your own weirdness.

FULL MOON *completion, fulfillment, abundance*

WANING GIBBOUS *review, reflection, introspection*

Pay attention to your dreams, because they have secrets to tell you under your eyelids. They will tell you things about your inner-most desires and your uncertain future, all glimmering in the distance. When you wake up, pay attention to how you feel in your muscles, to how your dreams are creating you. Let your dreams lead you outside your head and outside your door. Follow your desire down the street. It might feel like the universe is testing you in tiny, weird ways. It's only that the universe wants to see what you're made of and what you can really do when put to the test. Don't let yourself get frustrated; it wants to see you do well, to meet you halfway. The universe only wants to make you stronger.

Even while you keep changing, there's a version of you that you'll always come back to—the true you. Watch how the moon gets bigger but stays the same. Take a close look at these cycles and echoes of your life that swell up over and over. This is a time for listening and for noticing. You might wonder what for—but you'll only know it when you hear it and see it. Pay close attention to the cracks in the sidewalk, to the murmurs on the bus. Noticing these kinds of things takes practice and patience. It means moving deliberately through the world. Look up at how slowly the stars move across the sky; try to watch your plants grow. Try to rehearse their movements, practicing a strange kind of patience.

LAST QUARTER *discarding, amends, adjustment*

Let all your wayward sadness and crooked issues leak out of you like a deflated balloon. Keep talking until all the fears inside you have floated away. Think of everyone else as a sponge and yourself as spilled water. Your days might bend in strange new ways, and you might notice new kinds of light on your windowsill. You might feel the shape of your own life start to vibrate and shift. Let this happen. By giving in to change, the truth of who you are will stay solid and real. You won't desert yourself. Take a picture out your window each day and see what the smallest changes you can spot are. Remember that you, too, are changing in small and profound ways you won't be able to see for some time.

WANING CRESCENT *transition, healing, closure*

Be open to the possibility that your desires are changing shape. Be honest about the contents of your own heart. It's okay to throw dusty old dreams in the trash and to let go of old tattered hurts you're still clutching. Give yourself time to sink into this expansion, this strange new length. Let your body get used to this new atmosphere. You might feel a little unsteady, so go slow. It's easy to doubt the tug of your heart, to give in to the voices that tell you to be careful. It means that you're changing and shifting and that the new parts of you have yet to be named. Your feelings are wild and scary sometimes, and this is a time for listening to them and giving them a place to go. How do they want to express themselves?

Mood Phase Horoscopes

ROMANCE

What is water but a symbiotic merging of water and creatures? There's a part of you that is so at home in this desire to become one with another. For you, love can be an intangible thing that permeates your very existence. The consequence of this is that love happens in the real world in palpable ways. It can't live inside dreams forever; it needs the oxygen of two people loving and fighting and failing and trying. Try to see the ways in which you sometimes seek to be rescued from yourself—a seemingly impossible task, because there is always a you that you will have to return to. Practice the art of being present even when it's uncomfortable; try to recognize another person's failings as their tender humanity.

FEAR

There's a part of you with fears that aren't so much tangible as unknowable, which can make their shadows all the more terrifying. Because it's harder to see them head-on, you can be prone to escape the shapes they make on the walls of your mind by running as fast as you can in the opposite direction toward whichever escape you can find. The next time you get spooked, try drawing your fears into concrete shapes, blobby demons, or sad-eyed ghosts. Give them little thought bubbles and fill in what they want to say to you. Then write a list of all the things that define you. Remind your little blobs and ghosts that they have no jurisdiction over these definitions.

REFLECTION

There's a difference between reflecting on the past for the lessons you have learned and retreating to the past so it can serve as an unchanging refuge. The next time you find yourself dwelling on the past, pause to ask yourself which tactic you are taking. It's not always so black and white, but if your thinking is tinged with nostalgia, it's a sign that you might need more distance before you can get a clear view of it. One of your talents is the ability to intuit the connections and ties between people and to notice the things that remain unsaid. Allowing yourself to pause and reflect can help your own sense of definition and give you a clear before and after as a measuring stick.

STAGNATION

It's easy to get lost when the world is so full of bottomless emotions. You can split yourself easily between your thinking mind and your intuition. You can sense the deep connection between your physicality and your thoughts. Let that recognition guide you in the moments you feel lost. When you find yourself occupying the space above you rather than in your own physical sensations, put yourself back into the world. Write a list of the things that give you a sense of purpose in the world, from the tiniest to the biggest, from the most concrete to the most abstract. Look at the list whenever you need to be reminded of your worth and the direction the world is pointing you in.

ACTION

There is a part of you that is hyperconnected to your dreams and what they have to show you about yourself and the world. Your receptivity is a gift, both to yourself and others. It allows you to tap into energies, dualities, and worlds that other people can't access so readily. Give space to your dreams, paint them, write them letters, compose songs about them, and find their corollaries in the real world. This means that sometimes you'll need to give yourself the space to allow them to take hold, to whisper things to you that are important to hear. Practice keeping one foot grounded in the real world, by moving your body and connecting with others in a tangible way.

CHANGE

It's important to remember that perceived weaknesses are merely opportunities to redefine yourself, to find the version of yourself you'd most like to be. An opportunity for you to move toward an expanded sense of self is to practice staying put when you'd rather flee—both physically and mentally. This part of you can be slippery like a fish, both in your commitments to yourself and to others. Make a list of the times in your life when you've showed up, even when it scared you or it didn't turn out the way you wanted. Let this list be a constant reminder of your strength. When you can grind down into the ways in which you are solid, it's less easy for you to run away from that truth.

COMPASSION

This part of your elemental sensitivity and attunement to the subtleties around you make you an infinitely compassionate person. You withhold judgment because you truly understand what it's like to have fuzzy boundaries and to seek escape when the going gets rough. When you can focus this compassion on the world around you, it helps define your sense of self and exercises your innate wisdom and patience. It's important, however, to be alert to the ways in which your easy and inviting nature can attract those who would take advantage of it. Knowing where you end and the rest of the world begins can help you hone your intuitive sense of self. Practice drawing the outline of you on a piece of paper; color in the boundaries where everything else begins.

STRENGTH

This part of you is much stronger than you realize. Though you can be malleable, you have a quiet strength that reveals itself in your ability to listen and to take in what is happening around you without trying to change it. This is an ability that lends itself to empathetic endeavors, and it gives you the ability to be both completely open yet removed enough to withstand being walloped by waves of emotion. There's a part of you that can take in all the impressions and feelings and turn them into something wholly new, finishing what others can't. Let these gifts guide you toward your own understanding of your worth, to give you a direction to move toward and claim as your own.

Altar

This season, use your altar to honor your psychic and spiritual intuition.

Decorate your altar with ceruleans and teals, invoking the deep ocean.

Call upon fish of all kinds and all other creatures of the sea.

Place offerings of driftwood, coral, nautical ephemera, dream journals, healing salves, religious and spiritual items, poetry.

Charge your altar by illustrating a prayer to your subconscious.

Affirmations

I hold space and make time for those in need.

I offer my healing and empathy without letting it dissolve me.

I honor the wisdom of those who guide me, and I pass their gifts on.

I accept that in the end, we must all return to the dreamy depths.

Rituals

DREAM JOURNAL

This month, keep a pad of paper and pen next to your bed. Maybe you are someone who dreams and recalls dreams often. If you are not, that's okay; we will train this muscle. Each day, in addition to writing down what you remember from your slumber, record *how you felt* upon waking up. Take note of what state you are in before you go to bed and see if you notice any conditions that are most conducive to dreaming. Do you notice any parallels with what you are experiencing in waking life? What are your dream geographies like? Do you have recurring characters, locations, motifs, and themes? Are you ever able to tell yourself that you're in a dream? What things are dreams able to help you heal from? Write them down here.

INVENTORY OF FEELINGS

For the next week, you are to take a note every time you feel a feeling that is distinct and gives you pause. Also try to note the ones that you let pass through you like ghosts. Each time you notice one, don't write down the label you've given it in the past, but describe how it feels: What shape is it? What color? Where does it live inside you? Does it have a voice? What does it sound like? How does it behave? What happens when you breathe deep down into it? Give each of these feelings a name, the way you'd name a pet. Draw them and spend some time recording all the pertinent details. Do you notice any unexpected overlap, feelings that you label differently but seem to share similar attributes? When they show up again, see how your conversation with them changes.

About the Witches

Under a full moon in January 2014, Shewolfe and Beatrix Gravesguard beamed the first installment of *Astral Projection Radio Hour* on the radio waves of BFF.fm, a community station based in San Francisco. It soon became one of the most popular shows of the network, known for its conversational, authentic, and playful take on occult topics. Since the show's inception, they have observed a growing community hungry for a loose, interpretive, witchy spiritualism that parallels the rise of inter-sectional feminism, queerness, social justice, mental health awareness, self-care, and DIY culture in the face of an unpredictable world.

Notes of Gratitude

To our editor, Deanne Katz, and the Chronicle team for taking us on and guiding us through bringing our vision to life. To Kathleen Miller, for bringing Deanne our zine and setting the plans for this book in motion.

To our agent, Kate McKean, who during our first meeting told us her sun, moon, and rising signs without prompting. To Manjula Martin, who introduced us to Kate and imparted her book journey wisdom.

To Cosmic Amanda and BFF.fm for creating the community that conjured Shewolfe, Beatrix Gravesguard, and *Astral Projection Radio Hour* into existence.

To our parents and families for creating and nurturing our earthly apparitions. To Warlock Vic, the Decks & Noods coven, and our feline familiars, Roo and P'uddums, for their steady love and support.

And we thank each other for being copilots in this multidimensional friendship and collaboration, and sharing the immense effort, labor, and magic behind this book.

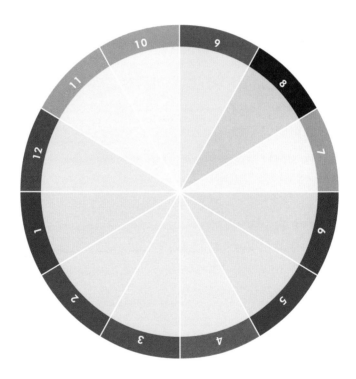

NAME: BIRTH TIME: BIRTH LOCATION:

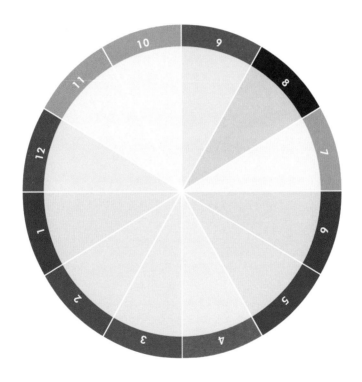

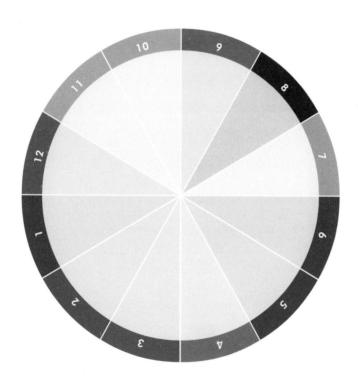

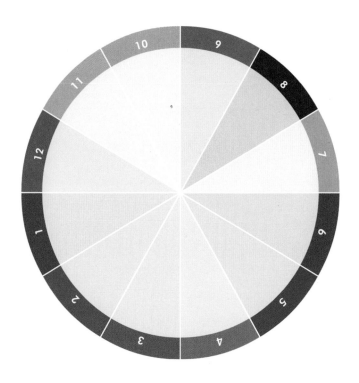

NAME: BIRTH TIME: BIRTH LOCATION:

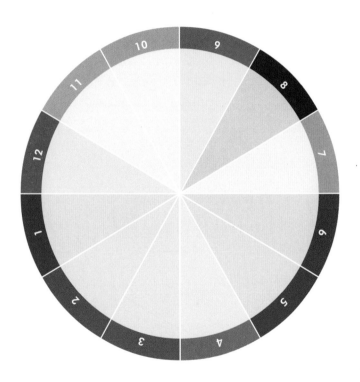

NAME: BIRTH TIME: BIRTH LOCATION:

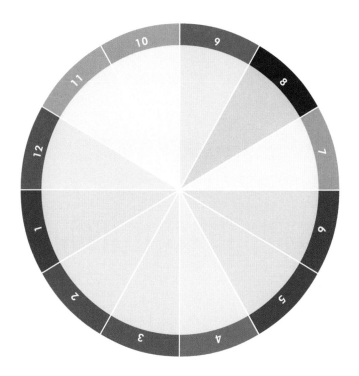

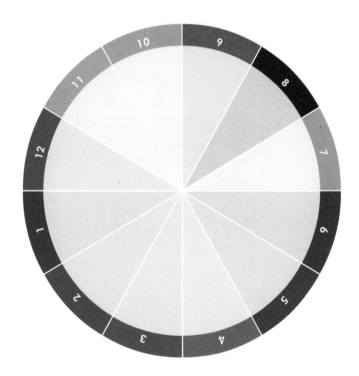